Where the Famous Lived in London

Christopher Mann

Photographs — Steve Lawrence
Drawings — Dacre Punt

The Serpentine Press Ltd.

This book is dedicated to Len Roxby —
who was a good friend and a true gentleman.

© 1974 The Serpentine Press

ISBN 0903961 00 8 (Paperback)
ISBN 0903961 01 6 (Hardback)

Page	Contents
6	Robert, Lord Baden-Powell of Gilwell
9	Aubrey Beardsley
11	William Bligh
14	Sir Winston Churchill
17	Robert, Lord Clive of India
21	Charles Dickens
24	Benjamin Disraeli, Earl of Beaconsfield
28	George Eliot (Mary Ann Evans)
31	Benjamin Franklin
34	Sigmund Freud
36	Mohandas Karamchand Gandhi (Mahatma)
39	David Garrick
41	Sir William Schwenk Gilbert
43	William Ewart Gladstone
46	Georg Friedrich Handel
49	John Fitzgerald Kennedy
52	Rudyard Kipling
55	Horatio, Earl Kitchener
58	T. E. Lawrence (Lawrence of Arabia)
61	Wolfgang Amadeus Mozart
64	Horatio, Viscount Nelson
67	Sir Isaac Newton
70	Samuel Pepys
73	William Pitt (The Younger)
77	George Bernard Shaw
79	Mark Twain (Samuel Langhorne Clemens)
81	H. G. Wells
84	James Abbott McNeill Whistler
88	William Wilberforce
90	Oscar Wilde
93	Map

ALBERT COURT (NEAR ALBERT HALL) HOWARD CARTER ARCHÄOLOGE
Cumberland Terr. 50
(gegenüber Regent Park)
opäts
Hampstead, Cannon House (Tusmuchs) Daphne du Maurier

Acknowledgements

Most of the houses included in this book have blue plaques erected by the Greater London Council or by its predecessor the L.C.C. A complete list of these houses is available in the booklet *Blue Plaques,* produced by the G.L.C.

Much of the information on the houses was obtained from the archives of the Greater London Council and grateful thanks are due to the Head Archivist, Miss E. D. Mercer, and to John Phillips, the Historical Research Assistant responsible for the G.L.C. commemorative plaques scheme, without whose unstinting help and encouragement *Where the Famous Lived in London* could never have been produced. I should also like to thank Lise-Lotte Guyatt and Barbara Angell for their research work, and Helen Steadman who acted as editor and proof-reader.

Preface

For a book entitled *Where the Famous Lived in London* the reader could justifiably comment that half the prose is taken up with the 'people' rather than 'where they lived'. I make no apologies for this.

For me, the fascination of the houses described and illustrated in these pages is not just that Nelson, or Kennedy, or Wilde lived there, *but what part these houses played in their lives and their life style.*

Thus to give you, the reader, a better appreciation of just what part these houses played in the lives of their famous occupants, I have described them in the biographical context of each of the individuals concerned.

Many of the houses included are relatively modest establishments, certainly not included in the 'architectural landmarks' of London.

Almost without exception, however, they have small details, points of interest which have been delightfully emphasised in the illustrations by Dacre Punt. His drawings give an extra fascination to some superficially quite drab buildings.

The many superb photographs were taken by Steve Lawrence, who went to great pains, getting up at unearthly times of day, to obtain shots of the houses whilst they were not obscured by passing traffic and parked cars so that the reader could envisage each house and its surroundings almost as it originally was.

Robert, Lord Baden-Powell of Gilwell

9 Hyde Park Gate, SW7

Robert Stephenson Smythe Baden-Powell was born at No.6 Stanhope Street, a four storey building in Paddington (now demolished). Robert's father, an Oxford don, died when Robert was only three years old, and Mrs. Baden-Powell discovered to her surprise that the Stanhope Street house was not in fact owned by the family. Her husband had, however, owned a house in Broom Hill and by selling it she was able to purchase for £6,200 Nos. 1 and 2 (now 9) Hyde Park Gate, to which the sizeable family now moved. There they were paid regular visits by W. M. Thackeray, John Ruskin, Robert Browning and other well-known figures in the literary world.

At the age of twelve, Robert Baden-Powell won a scholarship to Charterhouse and in 1876 took and passed the Army Examination with such distinction that he was given an immediate commission and posted to the 13th Hussars in India. Thus the young Baden-Powell found himself, somewhat surprisingly in view of his academic and literary background, embarking upon a military career.

Serving in India, Afghanistan and South Africa, his progress in the Army was rapid and by the time of the outbreak of the Boer War, he was the officer commanding British military operations in Matabeleland. He was responsible for the defence of Mafeking and successfully repulsed the Boers until its relief on May 17th 1900.

When the news of the relief of Mafeking reached England the unprecedented demonstrations of joy were such that a new word was coined

into the English language, 'Mafficking', meaning 'riotously exulting'! Baden-Powell, as one of the key figures, achieved almost overnight fame and was promoted to the rank of Major-General.

In 1878 Baden-Powell's mother left Hyde Park Gate and moved the family to 8 St. George's Place (now No.15 Knightsbridge). It was to this address that Baden-Powell returned during his short absence from active service, and it remained the family house until 1902, when the family again moved – this time to 32 Princes Gate.

At the termination of the Boer War, Baden-Powell was made responsible for the organisation of the South African constabulary.

On his return to England Baden-Powell went to live at Princes Gate and devoted himself to social work. His deep feeling for the under-privileged classes, together with his years of military training, took seed as he organised summer camps 'under canvas' for groups of working class boys on Brownsea Island in 1907: in the following year these were to become the beginnings of the Boy Scout Movement. Two years later, through his sister Agnes Baden-Powell, a similar organisation, the Girl Guides, was set up to cater for young girls.

In 1913, at the age of 56, Baden-Powell, a lifelong bachelor, got married. Soon after, the Baden-Powells gave up living in London and spent much of their time abroad. In recognition of his military services as well as his work with the Boy Scout Movement, which was rapidly achieving world-wide status, he was created a baronet in 1922 and a baron in 1929; he died and was buried in Kenya in 1941.

Of his residences in London both 9 Hyde Park Gate and 15 Knightsbridge (8 St. George's Place) still stand, although 32 Princes Gate has since been demolished. There is a Baden-Powell memorial plaque in Westminster Abbey and his wife, Lady Baden-Powell, still lives at Hampton Court Palace.

Tube: *Gloucester Road. Piccadilly, Circle and District Lines.* (Walk up towards Hyde Park or take a No.49 bus.)

Aubrey Beardsley
114 Cambridge Street, SW1

Aubrey Beardsley's parents lived in Brighton, where he was born on 24th August 1872. In 1883 his family moved to London where, in the following year, young Aubrey appeared on stage as the 'infant musical phenomenon'.

At the age of 16 he started work in an architect's office. Soon afterwards, however, his artistic talent came to the notice of the famous English painter, Sir Edward Burne-Jones, who urged Beardsley to take up a career in art. Inspired by this advice, he enrolled at Westminster School of Art and gradually became known in artistic and literary circles.

In 1893 Beardsley took a house in Westminster, No.114 Cambridge Street. By this time his work was becoming well-known and his unconventional, modernistic style was the subject of much controversy. During the two-and-a-half years that Beardsley lived at Cambridge Street, he produced what have become his most famous works, the illustrations to Malory'a *Morte d'Arthur* and Oscar Wilde's *Salome*. Working at all hours, Beardsley produced over 350 individual designs for the Malory book.

For a short time Beardsley worked on Oscar Wilde's quarterly magazine *The Yellow Book*, but was forced to leave in the blaze of publicity surrounding Wilde's unfortunate court cases.

In 1895 the artist left Cambridge Street and leased No.57 Chester Street, but by the end of that year he had taken up a nomadic existence, seemingly careless of his rapidly deteriorating health.

The following year Aubrey Beardsley joined Arthur Aymons on *The Savoy Magazine*, illustrating Pope's *The Rape of the Lock* (first published in serial form by the magazine). Unfortunately, Beardsley's worsening health and recurring tubercular attacks resulted in *The Savoy Magazine* going out of publication after only eight issues.

He travelled to Paris where, in the first weeks of 1898, he produced what was destined to be his last work of note, the illustrations for a new edition of Ben Johnson's *Volpone*.

Years of self-neglect had caused the complete breakdown of Beardsley's health. In the final stages of consumption, Beardsley travelled from Paris to Mentone in the South of France, where on March 16th 1898 he died, at the age of 26.

Tube: *Victoria.* Victoria, Circle and District Lines. (A few minutes' walk down Wilton Road to Warwick Way.)
Bus: Down Buckingham Palace Road to the BOAC Terminal, and then walk down Sutherland Street to Warwick Way. Nos. 11 or 39.

William Bligh
100 Lambeth Road, SE1

William Bligh was born in 1754 in Cornwall, as befits an English sailor.

At the age of eighteen he sailed with Captain Cook on his second expedition, as sailing-master of the *Resolution*. On this voyage the breadfruit was first discovered by the English at Otaheite, one of the South-Sea Islands, and in 1787 Bligh was given the task of introducing the breadfruit to the West Indies, earning the nickname of 'Breadfruit Bligh'. At the end of the year, Lieutenant Bligh and his crew sailed in the *Bounty* for Otaheite, and stopped there for six months before setting off for the West Indies. The crew, demoralised by thirst and hunger, resentful at having had to leave Otaheite and the native women with whom many of them had formed liaisons, focused their frustations on their commander. Led by the master's mate Fletcher Christian, they mutinied, and Bligh, with eighteen loyal crew members, was set adrift in an open boat.

The mutineers made for Pitcairn Island where they settled (and where their descendants live to the present day). William Bligh and his companions, after drifting for 4,000 miles and suffering badly from exposure, thirst and hunger, landed at Timor.

Returning to England in 1790 Bligh was promoted to the rank of Captain and given command of the *Providence*. The following year he sailed on a second 'breadfruit' expedition, this time completing his earlier mission to introduce the fruit to the West Indies.

By 1794 Bligh, now back in England, had married and taken a house in Lambeth: 3 Durham Place (now 100 Lambeth Road).

In 1797 he took part in the battle of Camperdown and in 1801, as commander of the *Glatton*, received a personal commendation from Nelson for his handling of the ship during the battle of Copenhagen.

Four years later Bligh was appointed

Captain General and Governor of New South Wales. He left his wife and younger children at the house in Lambeth and sailed with his daughter and son-in-law to Australia in February 1806.

Bligh, a completely honest and sincere man, nevertheless had an uncanny facility for stirring up resentment through his stubborn authoritarianism. In January 1808, less than two years after taking up his New South Wales governorship, he was again the centre of a mutiny, this time led by an infantry officer, Major George Johnston. Bligh was imprisoned by the mutineers and was not freed until 1810.

A letter, written from 3 Durham Place and dated August 1808 still exists: it was from Elizabeth, Bligh's wife, to her husband, and it accompanied a box containing among other things clothes, food, shoes, newspapers and magazines. Mrs. Bligh wrote at the end of the letter '... *this box I hope you will receive safe with my most sincere and affectionate Love. The Dear Children send their affectionate Duty — And I am, my dear Mr. Bligh most sincerely your Elizabeth Bligh.*' Obviously the fearsome Captain Bligh was regarded with love and affection within his family circle.

The New South Wales mutiny was overcome in 1810 and in 1811 Bligh returned once more to Durham Place and his family. He remained at Lambeth until his death in 1817 and was buried in St. Mary's Churchyard, Lambeth, where his tomb may still be seen.

⊖ **Tube:** *Lambeth North.* Bakerloo Line. (A short walk into Lambeth Road.)
Bus: Nos. 3, 10A, 44 or 159.

Sir Winston Churchill
28 Hyde Park Gate, SW7

Most people regard Winston Churchill, indisputably the most dominant British politician of this century, as the archetypal Englishman. He was, in fact, half American. The only child of the brilliant but erratic Lord Randolph Churchill and the beautiful American heiress Jennie Jerome, he was born at Blenheim Palace on November 30th 1874.

A reluctant and singularly unsuccessful pupil of Harrow School, Winston managed to scrape through the entrance examination to the Royal Military College, Sandhurst, at his third attempt, and in 1895, the year of his father's death, Churchill graduated from Sandhurst, a surprising 20th out of a class of 130.

The English language had already captured his imagination, and for the next five years he was to combine his military and literary talents as a soldier and war correspondent. He took part in the last-ever classical cavalry charge at the Battle of Omdurman in 1897, and in 1899, whilst serving as a war correspondent for the *Morning Post*, Churchill was captured by the Boers. He escaped, fleeing to Natal with a price of £25 on his head. During this time he wrote several books, including *Savrola*, a novel, and *The River War*, which described his own military experiences.

Returning to England, he entered Parliament in 1901 as Conservative Member for Oldham, but in 1904 resigned from the party. In 1906, as a Liberal candidate, he was elected M.P. for N.W. Manchester, and from 1908 to 1918 he was Member for Dundee.

In 1908 he had married Clementine Ogilvy Hozier, and it can justifiably be said that the unflagging support given to Churchill by his wife was a major factor in the success of his political and literary career.

In the same year he had become President of the Board of Trade and was instrumental in forming the basis of the modern welfare state. In the heated dispute over the radical Liberal budget of 1909, he was subjected to venomous attacks from the Tories and accused of being a traitor to his class. In 1910, Churchill, by now one of Lloyd George's most trusted aides, was made Home Secretary and between 1911 and 1915, as First Lord of the Admiralty, he was responsible for the rapid modernisation of the British Navy. Then in 1915 a wartime coalition was formed and the Tories insisted that Churchill, whose Dardanelles campaign had been a failure, be dropped from the government. Out of office, Churchill immediately volunteered for active service and for a time commanded the 6th Royal Scots Fusiliers on the Western Front. He was, however, soon recalled by Lloyd George and became Minister for Munitions and subsequently Secretary of State for War. After the war he was given the Air Ministry and before losing his seat in the 1922 election he had also become Secretary of State for the Colonies.

After toying with 'Independent Anti-Socialist' politics, Churchill returned to the Conservative party in 1924, and became Chancellor of the Exchequer under Stanley Baldwin. Acting on the advice of ministry 'experts', and against his better judgement, he returned Britain to the gold standard. This policy proved to be a disaster, and was one of Churchill's most serious political mistakes.

In 1929 the Tory government fell, and Churchill was to spend the next ten years out of office. He returned to writing and produced a massive biography of his ancestor, the Duke of Marlborough. He found relaxation in painting at his beautiful country estate and he became a proficient bricklayer.

In the thirties Churchill became increasingly alarmed at the rapid rise to power of the Nazis, and he was a vociferous and outspoken critic of the British Government's complacent attitude to events in Germany. So unpopular were his views that he was kept out of the Conservative Government when it was returned to power in 1935, and in the following year he became even more unpopular with Baldwin when he championed the cause of Edward VIII during the Abdication Crisis.

However, with the declaration of war on September 3rd, 1939, Churchill's fortunes were dramatically reversed. The same day he was reappointed to his old post, the First Lord of the Admiralty. By the following May, Germany had successfully invaded the whole of Europe, France had capitulated and the British Expeditionary Force was trapped at Dunkirk. The Allies' fortunes were at their nadir, and on May 10th Chamberlain resigned. Churchill, after so long in a state of political limbo, became Prime Minister. By a miracle the British troops were evacuated from Dunkirk, and from that point onwards Churchill inspired the British people by his own example, by his great gift of oratory, his close association with Roosevelt, and his diplomatic handling of Stalin, so that many became convinced that an Allied victory was well-nigh inevitable.

In the General Election of 1945 the Conservative party was defeated, despite Churchill's immense personal popularity. As Prime Minister Churchill, of course, had the use of 10 Downing Street. Out of office he was left without a base in London. He therefore purchased No.28 Hyde Park Gate, a charming little town house, previously owned by a jockey named Seracold.

Without the pressures of high office upon him, Churchill was able to devote much of his time to writing his own six-volume account of World War II. He was still a major world figure, however, and it soon became obvious that 28 Hyde Park Gate, whilst being an ideal parliamentary pied-à-terre, was simply not big enough to entertain the friends, statesmen and public figures who regularly came to visit Churchill in London. Fortunately, the house next door, No.27 Hyde Park Gate, came onto the market, and Churchill was able to purchase it and have Nos.27 and 28 turned into a single, much bigger house more suited to his requirements.

In 1950 there was another General Election and Churchill returned to Downing Street. This meant that the Hyde Park Gate house was no longer needed, and it was let to the Spanish Ambassador until 1955, when it once again came into use as Churchill's London home. Although he spent an increasing amount of time at his country estate at Chartwell, where he was able to indulge his other great love, painting, Churchill remained an active politician, declining a peerage in order to retain his seat in the House of Commons, which he held until 1964. When he died, Churchill was mourned throughout the world, and his burial place at Bladon, near Blenheim Palace, has become a place of pilgrimage for countless numbers of people from all over the world.

Tube: *Gloucester Road.* Cross over Cromwell Road and turn right. Walk along Cromwell Road to Queens Gate. Turn left into Queens Gate and walk up to Kensington Road. Turn left along Kensington Road and Hyde Park Gate is on your left.
Bus: Nos. 9, 9A, 52 or 73. Ask for Hyde Park Gate.

Robert, Lord Clive of India

45 Berkeley Square, W1

Robert Clive was born on September 29th 1725 at Styche, the family estate near Market Drayton in Shropshire. Forty-nine years later on November 22nd 1774 he committed suicide at his London home, 45 Berkeley Square, in a fit of depression brought on by his increasing addiction to opium. In his comparatively short lifetime he had become one of the most famous figures in English history and was the founder of the British Empire in India.

As a child, Clive seems to have shown many of the characteristics that would today have labelled him a juvenile delinquent. His uncle Daniel Bayley, in whose house in Manchester, Hope Hall, Robert spent some of his childhood, wrote of Robert that he was 'out of measure addicted to fighting'.

Whilst at school at Market Drayton it is said that he obtained 'protection money' from local shop-keepers to ensure freedom from the window-breaking activities of himself and his schoolfellows!

From Market Drayton he went briefly to Merchant Taylors' School and later to a private school in Hemel Hempstead where he remained until the age of eighteen.

On leaving school Clive was made a clerk in the East India Company and was sent out to Madras, arriving late in 1744. Clive did not find himself suited to the routine of office work and in a bout of depression attempted to commit suicide. Fortunately the pistol failed to go off.

Clive however was not long for the office desk, for the English and French were each striving to win the allegiance of the Indian rulers, a power struggle which, shortly before Clive's arrival, flared into open war. The war was, at least temporarily, decided in favour of the French, their commander Admiral Labourdonnais capturing Madras in 1746. Clive, along with the rest of the English in Madras, became a prisoner of war but he was later able to escape in disguise to the British-held Fort St. David. Here he commenced his military career as an ensign. At the time the British were in a parlous military situation, as the weak and undermanned Fort of Trinchinopoly was under heavy seige by the French-backed Chanda-Sahib. Clive, in an inspired moment, conceived the simple but effective plan of making a diversionary attack upon Arcot, Chanda's capital in order to force him to raise the Siege of Trinchinopoly to defend Arcot.

Clive's plan was a complete success. Chanda-Sahib and his troops hurriedly decamped from Trinchinopoly only to find that the British had occupied Arcot. During a siege lasting fifty-three days the British inflicted heavy casualties on the Franco-Indian force under Chanda's son Raja Sahib, and eventually forced them to withdraw. It was the turning point for the British in India and led, by 1752, to complete British control.

By this time Clive, whose bravery and skill had come to the fore when the British military reputation was at its lowest ebb, had won fame both in India and in England, where he returned in 1753 to recover from ill-health caused by the rigours of campaign and climate.

On his return, Clive, for the first time, stayed in London. He had acquired a considerable fortune in prize money and was able to bail his father out from financial difficulties. At this time he married Margaret Maskeyleyne in what was, surprisingly, to prove a lasting and happy union.

Clive never believed in half measures and by 1755 he had managed to dissipate the whole of his wealth and

was forced to return to India. He was appointed Governor of Fort St. David. Faced with the outrage of the Black Hole of Calcutta and the fall of Madras, Clive determined to overthrow the Indian ruler Siraj-ud-daula. On June 23rd 1753 Clive's force of 3,200 troops and nine guns smashed Siraj-ud-daula's army of 50,000 troops and 53 guns, for the loss of less than 80 men.

He returned to England in 1760 a rich man, having achieved international fame for his brilliant victory at Plassey. He stayed for a time at Swithins Lane (an address also used by his father) until, in the autumn of 1761, he purchased No.45 Berkeley Square from the Earl of Ancram. It was described in Gleig's *Life of Lord Clive* as 'The spacious house ... in which, till very lately his descendants continued to reside, he purchased on a lease of ninety years and fitted it up in a style of oriental magnificence.'

The following year he was given an Irish peerage with the title Baron Clive of Plassey and in 1764 was created a Knight of the Bath. As well as the house in Berkeley Square Clive had purchased an estate at Montfort near Shrewsbury. He became MP for Shrewsbury and was a strong parliamentary protagonist for the reform of both civil and military administration in India.

At this time, the British East India Company's interests in India were in a state of flux, and on June 4th 1764 Clive left England for Calcutta, arriving on May 3rd the following year. Confusion reigned; however, in a period of under five years, Clive restored the administration, boosted morale, transformed the operational efficiency of the British East India Company and extended British rule over the native states. It was a triumph of diplomacy and statesmanship unsurpassed in the whole history of the British Empire, achieved against a background of corruption and non-cooperation from both the British and the native rulers.

His task completed, he left Calcutta on the 29th January 1767. Once again he was received in England with joy, but there were undercurrents. He had many powerful enemies who formed a cabal against him, accusing him of corrupt dealings and accepting huge bribes in the form of gifts whilst in India. A parliamentary enquiry ensued, which uncovered evidence of corruption amongst employees of the East India Company and, by implication, indicated Clive as the fountainhead of the perfidy. Clive brilliantly defended himself in Parliament against the allegations; his name was cleared and after a night-long debate it was resolved that Clive had 'rendered great and meritorious services to his country'.

The strain, however, was more than Clive's melancholic temperament could take. He turned increasingly to opium for solace and on November 22nd 1774, in the house at Berkeley Square, he took his own life.

Clive's wife remained at 45 Berkeley Square long after his death and the house passed to his eldest son, Edward, who had become Earl of Powis. Around 1830 Edward had an extra storey added to the house but otherwise it remains little altered from the years of Clive's residence, and until the early years of this century the house remained in the hands of the Powis family, Clive's descendants.

Tube: *Green Park.* Victoria and Piccadilly Lines.
Bond Street. Central Line.
(A short walk from both stations.)
Bus: No.25.

Doorway of 45 Berkeley Square – Lord Clive's home between 1761 and 1774.

Charles Dickens
48 Doughty Street, St. Pancras W.C.1

Charles Dickens was born on 7th February 1812 at Mile End Terrace, Portsea, Near Portsmouth, Hampshire, second of the eight children of John and Elizabeth Dickens.

The Dickens family spent the years 1816 to 1821 in Ordnance Terrace, Chatham, where they were 'surrounded by soldiers, sailors, Jews, chalk, shrimps, officers and dockyard men'. In 1823 they returned to London, and they lodged briefly at a run-down house in Bayham Street, Camden Town, from whence, after falling into debt, John Dickens was removed to the Marshalsea prison. In order to make ends meet, Elizabeth Dickens opened an 'Educational Establishment' in Upper Gower Street, while Charles started work in a blacking factory. His soul-destroying work, together with the Christmas visits to his father at the Marshalsea 'hulks' had a profound effect upon the boy. The prison was later described in *The Pickwick Papers*, and the character of Mr. Micawber in *David Copperfield* was clearly based upon his father.

As with Mr. Micawber, 'something turned up' for John Dickens. A small inheritance freed him from the debtors' prison and Charles from the blacking factory.

After returning to school for two years, Charles started work in May 1827 with a solicitor, Mr. Blackmore, in Gray's Inn Road. During this time he lived with his parents at 13 Cranleigh Street, NW1, 10 Norfolk Street (now 22 Cleveland Street), W1, 15 (now 25) Fitzroy Street, W1, and finally Bentinck Street, Manchester Square.

Whilst at Blackmore's Charles taught himself shorthand and spent long hours at the British Museum, and in November 1828 he left the solicitor's office to become a reporter. By 1834 he was, in addition to his regular reporting duties, writing magazine articles, his *Sketches by Boz* appearing in *The Old Monthly Magazine* during that year.

On 2nd April 1836 he married Catherine Hogarth, and the following year *The Pickwick Papers* appeared in book form and was a runaway success. He moved with his wife into 12 (now 48) Doughty Street, St. Pancras, where they spent the next two years, during which time *Oliver Twist* was completed and *Barnaby Rudge* and *Nicholas Nickleby* begun. On leaving Doughty Street they moved into No.1 Devonshire Terrace, which was to be their home until 1851. This house unfortunately was demolished in 1958.

Returning to England after a tour of America in 1842 he completed *Master Humphrey's Clock*, which he had started in America.

In spite of the enormous success of his books, Dickens had been living beyond his means, and in order to meet his debts he wrote *A Christmas Carol* at the end of 1843. His output of consistently successful novels continued with *Dombey and Son, David Copperfield, Bleak House, Hard Times* and *A Tale of Two Cities*. For a time in 1846 he returned briefly to journalism as editor of the *Daily News*.

His marriage was not happy, and in

1856 he and his wife separated. Two years later, Dickens realised a childhood ambition when he bought Gads Hill House, near Rochester, Kent. It still stands, and is now a Dickens Museum.

He continued to spend much of his time in London, and early in 1861 he took furnished rooms at 3 Hanover Terrace, Marylebone, where he wrote most of *Great Expectations*.

Dickens made a second tour of America in November 1867, which earned him £20,000 but ruined his health. On his return to England he started work on his last novel, *Edwin Drood*, but before it was completed he died, at Gads Hill, on the 9th June 1870.

⊖ **Tube:** *Russell Square.* Piccadilly Line. (Walk down almost to the end of Gifford Street, then turn left.)
Bus: Nos. 45 or 259. (Down Gray's Inn Road, then get off at Guildford Street.)

Benjamin Disraeli, Earl of Beaconsfield

22 Theobalds Road, Holborn, WC1 and 19 Curzon Street W1

Benjamin Disraeli was born of Italian-Jewish ancestry on December 21st 1804 at No.22 Theobalds Road, although other addresses: St. Mary Axe, 6 Bloomsbury Square, the Adelphi and even 215 Upper Street, Islington (then Trinity Row) have since, at various times, been claimed as the scene of his birthplace.

Disraeli's father, Isaac D'Israeli, had taken the house two years earlier, and lived there with his family until 1817. A novelist, he wrote several books there. The house, which is still standing, has four storeys plus a basement and the original doorcase has a columned wooden porch. The original railings still enclose the front. A plain looking house, it seems it was redecorated and altered, possibly for D'Israeli, around 1800. The interior, still virtually as it was at the time of Benjamin Disraeli's birth and childhood, contains many original features of high architectural quality.

On leaving school at the age of 17 Benjamin Disraeli spent three years as an articled clerk to a solicitor, but decided against a legal career and decided to seek his fortune by gambling on the stock market. Not surprisingly this too was doomed to failure and by 1825 he was heavily in debt. Turning to journalism he subsequently wrote a romantic novel, *Vivian Grey,* which was published in 1826 and met with commercial success if not literary acclaim.

Fortunately for Benjamin Disraeli's future political career, his father, in 1813, quarrelled with officials of his synagogue (Jews were not at that time eligible for Parliament), severed his connection with the Jewish religion and had his four children baptised, Benjamin's christening taking place at St. Andrew's Church in Holborn in 1817.

The D'Israelis had left Theobalds Road in 1818 and moved to No.6 Bloomsbury Square, where they lived until about 1826 when Benjamin's father took a country estate, Bradenham Manor, situated at the foot of the Chilterns.

After a short tour of Italy Disraeli published two further novels, *The Voyage of Captain Popanilla* and *The Young Duke,* the money from which enabled him to make a two-year journey to Europe and the Middle East — a journey which was to have a profound effect upon his later political policies.

On his return in 1832 Disraeli decided to go into politics. After unsuccessfully standing no less than four times at High Wycombe and once at Taunton, he was finally returned as Conservative member for Maidstone in 1837.

During this period, in which his career as a political and romantic novelist flourished, Disraeli resided briefly at Duke Street, 31a Park Street, Grosvenor Square, and 34 Upper Grosvenor Street.

His maiden speech in Parliament on December 7th 1837 was a disaster, his affected modes of speaking and dress being ridiculed by other members. He was not deterred, however, and soon acquired the art of speaking in the House, eventually becoming one of its greatest orators.

In 1839 he married the widow of his fellow MP for Maidstone, Mrs. Wyndham Lewis, a lady of considerable fortune some twelve years his senior. After the marriage, Disraeli and his wife lived at No.1 Grosvenor Gate (now 29 Park Lane), a large and imposing house owned by

24

the former Mrs. Lewis, which remained Disraeli's home until his wife's death in 1872.

Between 1841 and 1847 Disraeli was MP for Shrewsbury, then exchanging the seat for that of Buckinghamshire which he retained until 1876.

Disraeli was rapidly gaining stature as a politician and in 1848 he became Leader of the House of Commons and in 1852, after the collapse of Russell's government, was made Chancellor of the Exchequer under the Earl of Derby. It was, however, a tottering administration which was defeated in December over Disraeli's budgetary proposals.

In 1858, after six years out of office, the Tories were returned to power under Derby, Disraeli assuming his earlier roles of Leader of the House and Chancellor. This administration too was defeated the following year, over a Bill to enfranchise more voters by broadening the voting qualification (which it seemed was not sufficiently radical) and Palmerston returned to the Premiership which he held until his death in 1865.

Returned to office the following year, the Earl of Derby once again appointed Disraeli as Chancellor and once again Disraeli attempted to introduce his voting reform, and this time, after a series of false starts, the Bill was eventually passed in August 1867. In February 1868 Lord Derby retired and Disraeli succeeded to the Premiership. A less than grateful nation, however, ejected the Disraeli administration in the same Autumn and once again the Liberals came to power, this time until 1874.

In 1848 Disraeli had purchased, in addition to his London home, a delightful country estate, Hughenden Manor, situated in the Chilterns near High Wycombe. The estate, still intact, remained in the family until comparatively recently and the house, quite small by the standards of the day, but delightfully situated overlooking a picturesque valley and unspoiled pastureland, is now a Disraeli museum.

In 1872 his wife Mary, who had shortly before been created Viscountess Beaconsfield, died. With her death came the loss of the Grosvenor Gate (Park Lane) house. The years spent by Disraeli in this house encompassed his progress from a young inexperienced Tory MP to Prime Minister of Great Britain. He wrote many of his books at Grosvenor Gate, including the novels *Coningsby* (1844), *Sybil* (1845), *Tancred* (1847) and his *Life of Lord George Bentinck* published in 1852.

On leaving 1 Grosvenor Gate, which, as 29 Park Lane, remains today little altered from the time of his occupation, Disraeli moved to 2 Whitehall Gardens and waited for Gladstone's government to complete its advancing process of self-destruction, which it duly did in 1874. In the ensuing election Disraeli polled a huge majority and was able to gather together a strong cabinet, as well as the unqualified support of Queen Victoria who had fallen under the spell of his charm and his extravagant (though probably sincere) flattery.

In 1876 Disraeli set the seal on his royal patronage by obtaining the title 'Empress of India' for Her Most Gracious Majesty. The previous year had seen Disraeli's crowning, and almost entirely personal, political achievement, the purchase from the financially tottering Khedive of Egypt of 177,000 shares in the Suez Canal. Hearing that the shares were to become available, Disraeli, on his own initiative, borrowed £4 million from his friends the Rothschilds and (presumably) crossed his fingers in the hope that Parliament would approve his bold move. Fortunately they did, and in retrospect, it is clear that Britain's interest in the Suez Canal was one of the cornerstones of the nation's prosperity in the twentieth century.

On other fronts, however, things were beginning to look rather bleak for Disraeli's Tory government. In 1876 the confrontation between Turkey and

25

Russia, which had long been brewing, finally flared up. Disraeli, who had from the days of his youth been very pro-Turkish, got into rather deep water over his support of the Turkish government, which had crushed a Bulgarian revolt using quite unnecessarily barbarous measures. The Russians then started moving into the Near East, 'in the name of humanity' and in 1877 open war between Russia and Turkey broke out. Disraeli was convinced of the strategic importance of the Turkish Empire and was becoming increasingly perturbed by the Russian advances. Some of his senior cabinet members, however, were equally convinced of the folly of Britain's becoming involved in the war, and Lord Caernarvon, the Colonial Secretary, resigned, closely followed by the Foreign Secretary, Lord Derby.

On the other side, Disraeli, now the Earl of Beaconsfield, was being pressed by Queen Victoria, who, with a pathological hatred of the Russians, was making warlike noises and even threatening abdication.

Fortunately the British fleet which had previously been sent to Constantinople, made a suitably impressive show of strength and so Lord Salisbury, head of the India Office, was able to prevent the Russians from implementing the Treaty of San Stefano which they had dictated on their defeat of the Turks, and lay down terms more acceptable to the English. These terms were detailed at the month-long Berlin Congress, which commenced on June 13th, with the Lords Beaconsfield and Salisbury representing the English interest.

Returning to England after the signing of the Treaty, Disraeli and Salisbury were given a triumphant welcome, Beaconsfield asserting that he had obtained 'Peace with honour'.

Other problems, notably the Zulu massacre in South Africa and the domestic agricultural depression, beset the Tory government and in 1880 they were soundly defeated in the general election.

During the period of 1876–1880 Beaconsfield had no London home other than, of course, Downing Street and so, much of the time he was in London he put up with various friends, including Lord and Lady Salisbury and the Rothschilds.

When he had taken the Premiership in 1874 his novel *Endymion* was half finished. On leaving office Lord Beaconsfield lived for a short time in Charles Street, Grosvenor Square. During his stay there he completed the book in order to provide the money to buy himself a house. As Concelle, a French biographer states: *'Il résolut d'acheter une maison à Londres tout près du Parlement. C'était pour lui chose dificile, car il manquait d'argent. 'Endymion' lui rapporte 250,000 francs (£10,000). Avec cela il acheta sa maison calle où il devait mourir.'*

This house was 19 Curzon Street, and he was able to secure a nine year lease which, as he commented to a friend, "I think will see me out".

In fact Beaconsfield was to live only nine months in the house: early in 1881 he caught a chill, his health rapidly deteriorated and on April 19th he died. During the last weeks of his illness Queen Victoria commanded that a layer of straw be laid in Curzon Street adjacent to Lord Beaconsfield's house in order that he should not be disturbed by passing carriages.

His funeral took place at Hughenden and Benjamin Disraeli, Earl of Beaconsfield, was buried in the family vault in the little church at Hughenden Manor.

Theobalds Road
Tube: *Holborn.* Central and Piccadilly Lines. (Over road up Southampton Row, first turning on left.)
Bus: Nos. 19, 38 or 172 along Theobalds Road.
Curzon Street
Tube: *Green Park.* Victoria and Piccadilly Lines. Walk down Bolton Street into Curzon Street.

George Eliot (Mary Ann Evans)
4 Cheyne Walk, SW3

Mary Ann (Marian) Evans was born on November 22nd 1819 at South Farm, Chilvers Coton, Warwickshire. Soon after her birth the family moved to Griff House, a rambling red brick farmhouse, and her childhood was spent in rural surroundings in which she delighted. At school she developed a great love of learning, but was subjected to a dogmatic Evangelical religionism which was to affect her throughout her life.

When she was twenty-two her widowed father retired to Foleshill, near Coventry. There Marian made friends with Charles and Caroline Bray and Charles Hennell, from whom she acquired the new and unorthodox religious views of the 'free-thinkers', and in 1843 she undertook a translation of Strauss' *Leben Jesu*.

Shortly after her father's death in 1849 she accepted the post of assistant editor of *The Westminster Review* and took lodgings in London at 142 Strand, a house owned by the *Review's* proprietor, John Chapman, until in October 1853 she moved to 21 Cambridge Street, Paddington.

In London Marian got to know many leading literary figures, including Carlyle, Newman, Spencer and George Henry Lewes. She and the already-married Lewes fell passionately in love, and despite censure the two lived together from 1854 in what was spiritually, if not legally, married bliss.

Because of prejudice against women writers, Marian published her first novel, *Amos Barton*, under the pseudonym 'George Eliot'. It appeared in *Blackwood's Magazine* in 1857 and was a success. It was followed in 1859 by *Adam Bede* which caused a sensation and established 'George Eliot' as one of the leading novelists of the day. The same year she and Lewes moved to 'Holly Lodge' in Wimbledon Park Road, Wandsworth. In 1860 and 1861 *The Mill on the Floss* and *Silas Marner* were published.

'Holly Lodge' was sold in 1860, and after 16 months in rooms at 10 Harwood Square, the couple leased No.16 Blandford Square until November 1863, when they bought 'The Priory', 21 North Bank, NW8, on a 49-year lease for £2,000, where they remained until December 1876, when they purchased 'The Heights' at Witley for £5,000.

Two years later, George Henry Lewes died. Marian, heartbroken, was helped through her grief by an old friend, Johnny Cross. After several proposals she eventually agreed to marry him, and on 10th April, 1880, they looked over 4 Cheyne Walk, Chelsea, a lovely old house adjacent to the river, and decided to purchase it.

The couple were married on 6th May 1880 at St. George's, Hanover Square. The evening before, Marian wrote to her friend Mrs. Burne-Jones:—

... We are going away tomorrow and shall be abroad two or three months. In August we shall be at Witley ... but this house will not again be my home. When in London we shall inhabit 4 Cheyne Walk, Chelsea.

After their return they did not move in to Cheyne Walk until December 3. Three weeks later, Marian caught a chill which developed into laryngitis. On December 22nd Marian Cross, known to millions of readers as 'George Eliot' the novelist, died. She was buried on the 29th December near to George Henry Lewes in a corner of Highgate Cemetery.

Tube: The nearest tube station is *Sloane Square*. Circle and District Lines.
Bus: The No.39 from Victoria goes to Cheyne Walk, although the service is fairly infrequent.

4 Cheyne Walk, where "George Eliot" died in 1880.

Benjamin Franklin
36 Craven Street, Westminster WC2

Born on January 6th 1706 in Boston, Massachusetts, Benjamin Franklin was the sixth son of Josiah and Abiah Franklin. Josiah, a dyer, had come from Banbury, in England, in 1685 with his wife and three children. In 1689 his first wife died and soon after he married Abiah Folger.

Benjamin left school at the age of ten to work for his father, now a tallow chandler. He had little interest in the job, so his father apprenticed the boy to his half-brother James, a printer. At the age of sixteen Benjamin began writing articles for his brother's newspaper, *The New England Courant*. Both the newspaper and Franklin's articles were a success, but he left for New York in October 1723 after a quarrel with James and subsequently went to England, arriving in London in December 1724. He first obtained a job at a printing firm, Palmers, later moving to another printer, Watts.

Franklin left England on July 21st 1726, having been offered a book-keeping job back in Philadelphia by a wealthy Quaker named Denham. His career as a book-keeper was brief, Denham dying a few months later. Returning to printing, Franklin purchased the *Pennsylvania Gazette* in 1729 and lifted it from mediocrity to the largest circulation in America. The following year he married Deborah Read; he already had a son, probably hers, and the couple later had two more children, Francis (who died in infancy of smallpox) and Sarah.

Benjamin Franklin's prosperity and diversity of interests rapidly increased, and by 1757 he was a man of wealth and stature and a politician of note.

That year Franklin returned to England, as agent for the state of Pennsylvania. He took lodgings with Margaret Stephenson at 36 Craven Street, Strand, on the recommendation of friends who had previously lodged there. He stayed with Mrs. Stephenson during the whole time he was in England, from 1757 to 1762, and after a brief return to the New World, between 1764 and 1775. He and Mrs. Stephenson became close friends (quite *how* close is a matter for conjecture!). Franklin

certainly showed little inclination to return to America, except in letters to his wife, to whom he wrote of London:

'The whole town in one great smoaky house and every street a chimney, the air full of floating sea coal soot, and you never get a sweet breath of what is pure without riding some miles for it in the country.'

Whilst in England Franklin received honorary degrees from the Universities of St. Andrews and Oxford. He had previously (in 1762) been elected a Fellow of the Royal Society for his scientific achievements, which included the discovery of the lightning conductor.

His later years in England were troubled, caught in the ever-widening rift between Britain and the Americas. He had become Deputy Post-Master General to the colonies and in 1773 he made a well-justified attempt to discredit Governor Hutchinson of Massachusetts, an American who, as an agent for the British, succeeded in alienating his countrymen from the British by his harsh and repressive acts. In this attempt, arch-royalist Franklin was hoping to revive British status in America. The British Government, however, took a dim view of his actions and in January 1774 he was dismissed from his post. He returned, somewhat disillusioned, to America in 1775, a new convert to American independence. Franklin's political career, however, had yet to reach its zenith: he took a major part in the preparation of the Declaration of Independence in 1776 and was four times elected president of the Commonwealth of Pennsylvania. Despite his failing health, Franklin became an ardent protagonist for the abolition of slavery and published several articles on this subject shortly before his death in Philadelphia on April 17th 1790.

Tube: *Charing Cross.* Circle, District, Bakerloo, Northern Lines. *Strand.* Northern Line. *Trafalgar Square.* Bakerloo Line.
Bus: Nos. 1, 6, 9, 11, 13, 15 or 77. (Get off at Charing Cross Station.)

Sigmund Freud
20 Maresfield Gardens, NW3

Sigmund Freud, the 'father' of modern psychoanalysis, was born at Frieburg in Moravia on May 6th 1856. When he was four his parents moved to Vienna, where Freud lived for seventy-eight years until the annexation of Austria by Nazi Germany in 1938. As a Jew, Freud was forced to flee the oppression of the Nazis. He took political refuge in London where, at 20 Maresfield Gardens, Hampstead, he found peace and sanctuary until his death on the 23rd September 1939.

As a young man Freud took more interest in scientific research than therapeutic medicine; however, after initially studying physiology and anatomy he subsequently turned to medicine. In 1886 he set up in practice as a neurologist, after a period in Paris studying under Jean Charcot. The key influence on Freud was, however, that of the Viennese researcher Josef Breuer from whom he learnt of the cure of a patient suffering from hysteria by the recall of the circumstances of its source under hypnosis. This became known as treatment by 'catharsis'. Freud developed this concept into the theory of 'free-association', foregoing hypnosis and encouraging the patient to talk freely on a wide range of subjects, eventually giving the clue to the patient's problems and identifying 'repressions' and their causes.

At the turn of the century Freud developed his new science much further by extensive analysis of his own sub-conscious, which he published as *The Interpretation of Dreams* in 1900.

Although met with much scepticism, Freud's work gradually became more widely accepted (especially in America), and in 1930 he received the Goethe prize.

After his escape from Nazi-occupied Austria he arrived in England with his family on the 6th June 1938. They stayed for a short time at a house in Elsworthy Road, NW3 (near Primrose Hill) before moving to 20 Maresfield Gardens, NW3, which was to be the Freuds' permanent residence.

Freud was able to have some of his furniture brought to England and so was surrounded at Maresfield Gardens by the comfortable familiar furnishings from his years in Vienna.

20 Maresfield Gardens is a large, dignified, many-windowed 'gentleman's residence', of a relatively simple style. At the rear of the house, the study overlooks an open loggia where the old man was able to relax in the open, protected from the wind.

In spite of his advanced years Freud remained remarkably active. He became a member of the British Psycho-Analytical Society, meanwhile continuing his writings in the Maresfield Gardens study. He produced, amongst other papers, *An Outline of Psycho-analysis,* as well as his last book, *Moses and Monotheism,* published in 1939.

He also continued to see patients, using the study as his consulting room.

In 1939 came a recurrence of the cancer that had first beset Freud sixteen years before, and on September 23rd, less than three weeks after the start of World War II, he died.

After Freud's death the house in Maresfield Gardens remained in the family and was lived in for many years by Anna Freud, the youngest of his six children and who had, herself, become a well-known psychoanalyst.

⊖ Tube: *Finchley Road.* Bakerloo and Metropolitan Lines. (Walk down Finchley Road, and Maresfield Gardens is on the left.)
Bus: Nos. 2, 2B, 13, 26, 113.

Mohandas Karamchand (Mahatma) Gandhi
Kingsley Hall, Powis Road, Poplar E.3

Mohandas Karamchand Gandhi was an anachronism: he lived through two world wars and a lifetime of economic, social and religious strife in his native India and yet was the supreme protagonist of peaceful resistance. He lived in an age of disillusion and yet he retained his high personal ideals and his faith in humanity throughout his long life.

He was born at Porbandar in Western India on October 2nd 1869, the son of a ruling-class Hindu family. As was the custom, Mohan was sent to London at the age of eighteen to complete his education and between 1878 and 1881 he studied law at the Inner Temple. Whilst a law student Mohan Gandhi lodged at several addresses in London, including 20 Baron's Court Road, 15 Charles Square and the house of Dr. Josiah Oldfield at 9 St. Stephen's Square (now 44 St. Stephen's Gardens).

He successfully completed his studies in 1881 and was called to the Bar; however he only practised in England for a short time and soon returned to India. After two not very successful years as a lawyer in India, he obtained a post with an Indian firm in South Africa. In South Africa Gandhi, already acutely conscious of the suffering of others, campaigned strongly for the political rights of the Indian minority there. He gave up his now lucrative legal practice and set up a self-dependent commune in order to devote himself full time to public work.

In the course of his struggle for the South African Indians, he suffered imprisonment, abuse and assault but throughout kept his dictum of peaceful dissent. By 1914 he had gained a considerable measure of success: many of the repressive acts against the Indians in South Africa had been repealed and Gandhi therefore returned to India.

He had now two aims in view: to achieve a rapprochement between the Hindus and Moslems, who had been at each others' throats since time immemorial; and to gain Home Rule for India. Despite his insistence on non-violent action some of his followers found themselves incapable of living up to Gandhi's high principles, with the result that violence erupted on several occasions. When this occurred Gandhi made personal penances to 'atone' for his followers' sins but in 1922 he was arrested and sentenced to six years' gaol. He was however released after serving only two years. He continued to fight for an understanding between the Hindus and Moslems as well as against the archaic 'caste' system which made outcasts of the 'untouchables'.

In 1927, the British government set up an 'independence' Commission. Progress was slow and a group of radicals started a campaign of violence against British rule. This brought the Mahatma (a term meaning great sage or philosopher) Gandhi back into the political arena and he began a strategy of non-violent civil disobedience which proved to be so successful that in 1930 he was once again imprisoned. At this time the British government set up a conference in London, attended by several Indian moderates, which made great progress towards Indian independence. Gandhi, who had been freed from prison, was persuaded to join the Indian delegation for the second independence conference in London late in 1931. Arriving in London, he stayed at Kingsley Hall, Powis Road, Poplar, E3, where he was a guest of Miss Muriel Lester, who was the

housewarden. Gandhi was in London for three months whilst the conference continued.

Since the previous conference England had had a general election and a change of government. All the progress made was nullified by the dogmatic stance of the new Ramsay Macdonald government. The Indian delegation returned home after a fruitless mission and were rapidly returned en masse to gaol.

Late in 1932 the British government published its Indian proposals, offering separate political representation for the 'untouchables'. This was intolerable to Gandhi who was morally outraged at the continued separation of the untouchables. He fasted in gaol until a compromise solution was found. From the time of his release until the start of World War II Gandhi threw himself wholeheartedly into the task of representing the untouchables in their struggle to achieve a degree of equality.

During the war years Gandhi exercised a moderating influence between the Indian Congress and the British government, but his more militant colleagues held sway and once again in 1944 Gandhi was placed under detention. During this detention both he and his wife became ill, and she died in February 1944. Gandhi, after his recovery a few months later, was released.

After the war there was again a change of government in England and the Indian dream of independence began to take reality. Gandhi, strongly opposed to the partition of India, desperately tried to reach an agreement with the Moslem leaders. However, the differences between Hindu and Moslem were too deeply etched to be resolved. The Moslem-Hindu dispute flared up into violence and in 1946 riots and mass killings on both sides took India to the brink of civil war.

Gandhi's dream of a united India had failed. Congress acceded to partition, and Independence was achieved on August 15th 1947. There followed an uneasy truce between the tribes, with violence erupting at the slightest provocation. Gandhi continued to strive for peace between the two religious factions although by this time he must have been suffering considerable disillusion. In January 1948, the situation between Hindu and Moslem had deteriorated to the extent that, in the largely Hindu town of Delhi, Moslems went in fear of their lives. In an attempt to persuade his fellow Hindus to live in harmony with the Moslems, Gandhi once again went on hunger strike until the Hindu leaders had promised to treat the Moslems as neighbours. His interference was, however, resented by some Hindus and ten days after the successful termination of his fast he was assassinated by a Hindu extremist whilst walking to a prayer meeting.

Kingsley Hall, where he stayed in London, is now a run-down semi-derelict building in the East End near to the docks. The room occupied by Gandhi still contains his portrait and other mementoes and some of his writings. The house somehow typifies his feeling for the under-privileged of every nation, his dignity and his rejection of humanity's material values for unshakeable spiritual principles.

Tube: *Bromley by Bow*. District and Metropolitan Lines. (Walk up St. Leonards Road to Grove Street or Bruce Road, and Powis Road is at the end of both.)
Bus: Nos. 86, 108, 52

David Garrick
27 Southampton Street, WC2

During the forty-two years Garrick spent in London he had three major residences: 27 Southampton Street, 5 Adelphi Terrace and 'Garrick's Villa' in Hampton, Middlesex.

He was born on February 19th 1717 at Hereford. His father, Captain Peter Garrick, was a soldier of French Huguenot descent and spent long periods away from home, during which he and 'little Davy' conducted a regular correspondence. David was educated at Lichfield Grammar School until July 1736, when he and his brother George were sent to Samuel Johnson's newly opened academy at Edial which, unfortunately, closed after only six months. Johnson and Garrick had, however, become friends and the two decided to seek their fortune in London. Soon after their arrival, Garrick's uncle, a wine merchant, died, leaving him £1,000. With this money he and his brother George set up a wine merchant's which met with little more success than Samuel Johnson's school and was closed down at the end of 1741.

By this time Garrick had acquired a fascination for the stage and began playing his first roles under the name of Lydall.

On October 19th 1741 he took the part of Richard III at Goodman's Fields and caused a sensation. By December he was performing under his own name and had set theatrical circles ablaze, Pope commenting: 'that young man never had his equal as an actor, and he will never have a rival'. His talent for writing as well as that for acting was confirmed soon after, when his farce, *The Lying Valet*, was a great success.

In 1747 he bought the Drury Lane Theatre with his partner Lacy, and became its manager until his retirement in 1776.

Garrick and his wife moved into No.27 Southampton Street, which was to remain the Garricks' London home until 1772.

'Garrick's Villa' at Hampton in Middlesex, then known as 'Fullers House', was bought by the actor/manager in 1754, at which time it comprised two houses. These Garrick made into one, adding a new façade designed by the Adam brothers. The Garricks used the house as their country home amd gave frequent, lavish parties and 'night fêtes'. Mrs. Delaney wrote of the villa that, 'on the whole it has the air of belonging to a genius', and Samuel Johnson, asked by Garrick what he thought of the place commented, 'Ah, David, it is the leaving of such places as these that makes a death bed terrible'.

Garrick was a generous contributor to many charitable causes and on the 1st of May each year he and Eva, 'the best of women and wives', opened the grounds of the villa and provided sweetmeats for all the local children.

Garrick, of course, still spent much of his time in London and, on leaving Southampton Street in 1772, he acquired No.5 Adelphi Terrace, which he kept until his death on January 20th 1779.

His wife survived him by forty years, and continued to live at the villa in Hampton. The house still stands, outwardly much as it was, but it has since been renovated and converted into flats.

🚇 **Tube:** *Covent Garden.* Piccadilly Line. (Walk down St. James Street, across Covent Garden Market and into Southampton Street.)
Bus: 1, 1A, 6, 9, 9A, 11, 13, 15, 77, 77A, 77C, 170, 176 to The Strand.

Sir William Schwenk Gilbert

39 Harrington Gardens, SW7

W. S. Gilbert was born in London on November 18th 1836. His father was a novelist, and William, a talented artist, illustrated several of his books.

He left school in 1857, and after a short period as a Civil Servant, studied law for three years and was called to the Bar in November 1864. Three years earlier he had begun contributing comic verses and humorous illustrations to the publication *Fun*, and in 1866 he deserted the law to become a dramatic critic for the *Illustrated Times*. Early in December of that year he was approached by T. W. Robertson to produce 'a bright Christmas piece within a fortnight'. Gilbert wrote *Dulcamara* within ten days, rehearsals took place the following week, and it was performed for Christmas. Gilbert had sold the work for £30, which was a mistake as it proved to be a great success.

In 1867 Gilbert married Agnes Lucy Metcalf, and in 1870 they moved to No.8 Essex Villas, Holland Park. Here he wrote the libretto to *Thespis* and *Trial by Jury*, the first operettas produced in collaboration with Sir Arthur Sullivan for the D'Oyly Carte Opera Company, and the start of a partnership which was to flourish for over twenty years.

Gilbert and his wife moved in 1876 to Bolton Street, where he wrote *H.M.S. Pinafore*, *The Pirates of Penzance*, *Iolanthe* and *Princess Ida*. He commenced *The Mikado* prior to moving to 39 Harrington Gardens, which the librettist had had specially built, in 1884. Here the work on *The Mikado* was completed, followed by *Ruddigore*, *The Yeoman of the Guard* and *The Gondoliers*.

Whilst at Harrington Gardens Gilbert organised children's parties, which became almost an institution, Gilbert romping and revelling with his small guests and obviously enjoying himself as much as the children. As well as the children's entertainments, he and his wife gave regular dinner parties at Harrington Gardens. He was 'a master of small talk'. At one dinner there was an uncomplimentary discussion about a large, matronly body. Gilbert remarked benignly: 'After all, she's quite nice, only I prefer a woman to be as long as she is broad!'.

On these occasions Gilbert always sat with a woman each side of him. Surrounded at one dinner by quite a crowd he was asked why he was inconstant. Gilbert beamed at the questioner and replied, 'Because I am too good to be true'.

After the appearance of *The Gondoliers* the relationship between Gilbert and Sullivan cooled somewhat, although their collaboration continued.

In 1890 Gilbert finally left Harrington Gardens and moved to Grim's Dyke, a fine house set in the beautiful rural surroundings of Harrow Weald. The house (now a hotel), was built by Norman Shaw for Frederick Goodall, who in 1882 sold it to a banker named Heriot.

On May 29th 1911, a young guest got into difficulties whilst swimming in the lake at Grim's Dyke. Gilbert, despite his seventy-four years, bravely dived in and rescued her. Unfortunately the strain proved too much: he had a heart attack and was drowned.

Tube: *South Kensington.* District, Circle and Piccadilly Lines. (A short walk from the station.)
Bus: Nos. 14, 30, 74 or 49. (49 actually goes down Harrington Road.)

A Gilbertian residence! 39, Harrington Gardens

William Ewart Gladstone

11 Carlton House Terrace, SW1

William Ewart Gladstone was the fourth son of John and Anne Gladstone. He was born on the 29th December 1809 at 62 Rodney Street, Liverpool and at the age of twelve was sent to Eton. After leaving Eton Gladstone went up to Christ Church College, Oxford. First secretary and then president of the Oxford Union, his eloquence was even then remarkable. Bishop Wordsworth thought that 'Gladstone, then our Christ Church undergraduate, would one day rise to be prime-minister of England'. In December 1831 he took a double first. The following year the Duke of Newcastle, whose son had heard Gladstone speak at the Oxford Union, invited him to stand for the Tory Party at Newark, and on the 29th January 1833, 24-year-old William Ewart Gladstone took his seat in the House of Commons and moved into chambers at the Albany.

His first term as an MP was fairly brief, as Parliament was dissolved on his 25th birthday, one month after his appointment to a Junior Lordship of the Treasury. At the following election, Gladstone was returned unopposed and was promoted to the Under-Secretaryship for the Colonies. On 30th March the government was defeated and Gladstone temporarily left the political arena.

The next few years were devoted to literary work and in 1838 *The State In Its Relations with the Church* was published. On July 25th 1839 Gladstone married Catherine Glynne, and gave up his rooms at the Albany to move into 13 Carlton House Terrace.

In the General Election of 1841 Gladstone returned to Parliament and the Prime Minister, Sir Robert Peel, appointed him Vice-President of the Board of Trade. Two years later Gladstone succeeded Lord Ripon as President, becoming a member of the Cabinet at the age of 33. He resigned office in 1845 and did not contest the election that year, but at Sir Robert Peel's request he became Secretary of State for the Colonies, which post he held until June 1846, when, after a government defeat, Peel resigned and Lord John Russell became Prime Minister. In 1847 Gladstone was re-elected to Parliament as a Member for Oxford University.

On August 17th 1848 he and his wife moved to 6 Carlton Gardens, where Gladstone's father had lived since 1836. He assigned the lease to William 'In consideration of a natural love and affection which I have for my son'.

In 1852 Benjamin Disraeli became Chancellor of the Exchequer for the Whig Government, a position which he held until the dissolution of Parliament on July 1st. His budget speech was vigorously opposed by Gladstone, and marked the beginning of a lifelong rivalry between the two men. A coalition government of Whigs and Peelites was formed, with Gladstone as Chancellor of the Exchequer. This post he retained until 1857, when soon after the resignation of Lord Aberdeen and the succession of Lord Palmerston, he resigned over a policy disagreement. The previous year, Gladstone had purchased the lease of No.11 Carlton House Terrace. The terrace had been built on the site of the gardens of the Prince Regent's residence, Carlton House. No.11 was a large and imposing house which had the principal rooms on the first floor, and these were probably used by Gladstone for receiving guests.

British politics at this time were in a state of ferment. Palmerston was succeeded by Lord Derby as Prime Minister, whilst Gladstone briefly became High Commissioner Extraordinary to the Ionian Islands. In the 1859 session, the government was defeated over the Reform Bill and

Parliament dissolved. Gladstone was returned unopposed for the University of Oxford. Lord Derby resigned and Palmerston again became Premier, re-appointing Gladstone Chancellor of the Exchequer. Some stability had returned and Palmerston retained office (as did Gladstone) until his death in 1865.

Palmerston was succeeded by Lord Russell, and Gladstone became Leader of the House as well as Chancellor of the Exchequer. In March 1867 the government was defeated in an attempt to introduce a moderate Reform Bill and Gladstone was, once again, out of office.

That Christmas Lord Russell retired from politics, bequeathing the leadership of the Liberal Party to Gladstone. On December 2nd 1868 the Tories, under Disraeli, were defeated over the Irish Question and for the first time Gladstone became Prime Minister.

His government, too, was finally defeated over Irish reforms and Parliament dissolved in January 1874. Gladstone was now 64 and giving thought to retirement, and in 1875 he resigned the leadership of the Liberal Party. The same year he sold the lease of 11 Carlton House Terrace and moved with his wife to 73 Harley Street, a house which was, unfortunately, demolished at the turn of the century.

In 1880 the Tories were soundly beaten in the General Election by the Liberals, and Gladstone was asked to become Prime Minister. He accepted and his second term of office ran until 1885, when the government was defeated over the budget. On his defeat Gladstone was offered an earldom by Queen Victoria, which he declined. In 1886, Gladstone became Prime Minister for the third time after a brief Tory administration. This third term as Prime Minister was destined to be even more brief. Parliament was dissolved after only seven months and in the election which followed the Tories, under Lord Salisbury, were returned with a majority of over 100.

In 1890 Gladstone left Harley Street and after a short stay at 16 St. James Street (now Buckingham Gate) made his London residence at 10 St. James's Square.

Gladstone became Prime Minister for a fourth time when the Tories were given a vote of no confidence in 1892. On 1st March 1894 Gladstone made his last Commons speech, two days before handing his resignation to the Queen. Even then he continued in public life until a short time before his death in his country house at Hawarden on 19th May 1898.

11 Carlton House Terrace is still much as it was during Gladstone's residence. A plaque was originally mooted for the house in 1907 but the then owner-occupier, Lord Ardilaun, refused permission for its erection. The plaque was eventually erected in 1925. After the refusal of Lord Ardilaun, Sir E. Durning Lawrence, the occupier of No.13 Carlton House Terrace, where

Gladstone had also lived, was approached for permission to allow a plaque to be erected there. This too was doomed to failure, Lawrence replying in a letter . . .
'I object very much to such being affixed to this house. Mr. Gladstone not only lived here but also at '11' and, I believe, in one or two other houses in this part and innumerable other houses in London.'

Tube: *Trafalgar Square.* Bakerloo Line. (A very short walk down the Mall.)
Bus: Buses do not run down the Mall. A few buses go *westward* along the one way system from Piccadilly and Trafalgar Square i.e. Nos. 9, 14, 506 etc.

Georg Friedrich Handel
25 Brook Street, W1

Georg Handel was a barber-surgeon of some note in Halle, Saxony. Here, on 23rd February 1685, his son Georg Friedrich was born. At an early age Georg Friedrich showed a prodigious musical talent. His father, however, intending him for the law, forbade him to have anything to do with music. Fortunately Duke Adolf I of Weissenfels heard the seven-year-old Georg playing the organ and was so impressed that he urged the boy's father to allow him a musical education. Thus Handel studied music as well as law, taking his law degree whilst earning a living as organist at the Halle Cathedral.

His first musical success was the opera *Almira,* produced in 1705. Travelling to Italy his fame became more widespread and in 1710 he was appointed 'Kapellmeister' to the Elector of Hanover. Shortly after the appointment, Handel requested leave to go to England. He liked England and had not long returned to Hanover when he obtained permission from the Elector to go back there, on the understanding that his stay would be short. Handel arrived in 1712, and the Duke of Chandos became his patron. At Canons, the Duke's residence in Edgware (now the famous North London Collegiate School) Handel

composed his first oratorio *Esther* and later the *Largo*.

In 1713 Queen Anne died and the Elector of Hanover became King George I of England. This placed Handel in an awkward situation as he was in disfavour at the Hanoverian court due to his prolonged absences in England. The King's approbation was regained, however, by the *Water Music* which Handel composed for a royal trip on the Thames.

In 1723 the composer purchased an elegant Queen Anne house, No.57 Brook Street, W1 (now No.25). At this house, in the music room on the first floor, Handel wrote some of his greatest works including *The Messiah* and *Israel in Egypt*.

By 1727 he had become a naturalised Englishman and had gained considerable popularity, although hostility from a rival operatic group led him in 1737 to bankruptcy and illness. In spite of his financial troubles, which were to recur in 1745, Handel's mode of living was not prodigal, in fact his only extravagance was good food and wine. At one of his frequent dinner parties, he exclaimed 'Oh, I haf de thought', and the guests, not wishing to disturb the great man's inspiration, urged him to another room to set down his thoughts. Subsequently these thoughts became increasingly frequent and it was eventually discovered that they were being bestowed upon some superior wine that he did not wish to share with his guests!

By 1751 Handel's sight was failing and by May 1752 he was almost blind. His last years were spent living and working at Brook Street where, on April 14th 1759, he died, only a few days after attending a performance of his *Messiah*.

25 Brook Street remains much as it was in 1759, although late in the 19th century an extra floor was added and, in 1906, the ground floor was converted into a shop. Between the wars there was an attempt to raise money to make the house London's Handel Museum. Unfortunately, only £250 was raised and the scheme was abandoned.

Tube: *Bond Street*. Central Line. (A short walk from the station down New Bond Street.)
Bus: No.25 up and down New Bond Street. Along Oxford Street: Nos. 1, 7, 8, 25, 73 and many others.

John Fitzgerald Kennedy
14 Princes Gate, South Kensington, SW7

Ireland in 1850 was a country beset by a disastrous potato famine. The effect of the famine on the Irish, for whom potatoes were a staple part of their diet, was beyond belief, with many families literally starving to death. It was this situation that caused Patrick Kennedy to emigrate from New Ross, County Wexford, to Boston, Massachusetts. His grandson Joseph Kennedy, on graduating from Harvard in 1912, entered the banking profession and by 1930 had by shrewdness and diligence become one of the richest men in America. By this time he had developed a great interest in politics and was an ardent supporter of Roosevelt during his successful campaign for the presidency in 1932. During Roosevelt's administration Joseph Kennedy was appointed to several important posts, culminating in the Ambassadorship to Great Britain in 1937.

The American Ambassador's residence in London was a large and imposing house, built round about 1850: No.14 Princes Gate. Originally built as two houses the property was bought in the early years of the twentieth century by a wealthy American banker, John Pierpoint Morgan (senior) who converted the two houses into one and made elaborate alterations to both the façade and interior.

It was to this house that Joseph P. Kennedy came to live in 1937. With him he bought his wife and several of his nine children, including Robert and Edward. John Fitzgerald Kennedy, however, was not in the 'Kennedy Ambassadorial team' as he was at this time a Harvard undergraduate, seemingly more interested in athletics than academic honours.

John F. joined his family in London early in 1939. His earlier interest in athletics was by now taking second place, and whilst living at Princes Gate he put the time to good use in studying for his degree and was, in fact, enrolled as a student at the London School of Economics. Frequent contact with the major contemporary political and diplomatic figures at Princes Gate, together with a quick and analytical brain, enabled him to write a concise and perceptive thesis which in the year after the Kennedys returned to America was published as a book, *Why England Slept*. It became a best-seller on both sides of the Atlantic. Kennedy graduated in 1940 and the following year was commissioned into the US Navy. He saw action against the Japanese in the Pacific and by the end of the war had won not only the Navy and Marine Corps Medal but also the coveted Purple Heart.

Returning to civilian life, Kennedy entered politics and late in 1946 was elected to the House of Representatives. His career as a Congressman was little short of meteoric and in 1952 he opposed Republican Henry Cabot

Lodge for the latter's Senate seat and against all odds, defeated him.

The following year the young senator married Jacqueline Lee Bouvier. Soon after he was forced to enter hospital for treatment to his spine which had been injured during the war. During the six months of his hospitalisation Kennedy wrote a second book, *Profiles in Courage,* which won the 1957 Pulitzer Prize for Literature.

Narrowly defeated in a bid to become Adlai Stevenson's vice-presidential running mate in the 1956 election, Kennedy lost little time in preparing himself for an all-out bid for the presidency in 1960. By the time of the elections, the young, gifted, handsome and wealthy senator had become one of the best known political figures in the United States. The Kennedys, husband, wife and family, formed a formidable political machine. During the 1960 Primaries he won every ballot he entered. The eventual election of Kennedy to the Presidency seemed an almost foregone conclusion, but in the November elections he defeated the Republican candidate Richard Nixon by only the narrowest of margins.

During the three short years of his presidency, John F. Kennedy embarked upon a domestic programme of social and economic reform. On an international front East/West relations were very strained and after an abortive CIA-inspired attempt to invade Cuba the situation became even worse. In August 1962 the Soviets erected the infamous 'Berlin Wall' which triggered off a war of nerves between the Russian leader Kruschev and Kennedy, culminating in the Cuban missiles crisis in October, when Kennedy called Kruschev's bluff and forced him to back down and withdraw Soviet missiles from Cuba.

On November 22nd 1963 as John Kennedy and his wife were travelling in a motorcade in Dallas, Texas, the President was shot and mortally wounded by an assassin. Probably no single death before or since has been the cause of more controversy. The alleged assassin, Lee Harvey Oswald, was himself murdered two days later, as he was being transferred from gaol, in front of millions of American TV viewers.

John Fitzgerald Kennedy, thirty-seventh President of the United States, was buried at Arlington Cemetery on November 25th amid scenes of unprecedented national mourning. Today, more than a decade later, the shock waves created by his assassination have yet to subside.

Tube: *Knightsbridge.* Piccadilly Line.
Bus: Along Knightsbridge and Kensington Road from Hyde Park Corner. Nos. 9, 9A, 52 or 73.

51

Rudyard Kipling
43 Villiers Street, WC2

Rudyard Kipling was born on December 30th 1865 in Bombay, where his father was Principal of the Mayo School of Art. Rudyard and his sister Beatrix were sent by their parents to England, where they were looked after by elderly relatives living at Southsea, Hampshire. Here the two children spent four years of unremitting misery until finally their mother arranged for them to stay with the Misses Craik, two elderly spinsters who lived in Warwick Gardens, Kensington.

When he was thirteen, Rudyard left London to go to the United Services College at Westward Ho, Devon, which was later to become the scene of one of his novels, *Stalky and Co.* Kipling left Westward Ho in 1882 and returned to India, where he took up the position of sub-editor for *The Civil and Military Gazette.* Something of a poet, Kipling wrote satirical verses for the *Gazette.* These were published as a collection, *Departmental Ditties,* in 1886 and proved to be a success. *Plain Tales from the Hills,* a collection of stories, again originally written for the *Gazette – Soldiers Three, The Story of the Gadsby* and *In Black and White* were published a year later. The same year Kipling became assistant editor of the *Allahabad Chronicle,* a job which entailed a great deal of travelling. After spending some time in America, he returned to London in September 1890 'with fewer pounds in his pocket than he cared to remember', and took lodgings in three rooms on the second floor of No. 43 Villiers Street. In his autobiography, *Something of Myself,* Kipling comments:

'Villiers Street ... *was primitive and passionate in its habits and population. My rooms were small, not over-clean or well kept, but from my desk I could look out of my window through the fan-light of Gatti's Music Hall entrance, across the street, almost on*

to its stage. The Charing Cross trains rumbled through my dreams on one side, the boom of the Strand on the other, while before my windows, Father Thames under the Shot Tower walked up and down with his traffic... My rooms were above an establishment of Harris, the Sausage King who, for tuppence, gave us as much sausage and mash as would carry us through from breakfast to dinner.'

During his stay in Villiers Street he wrote many articles and poems, as well as a novel, *The Light that Failed*. Kipling regularly frequented Gatti's and wrote of 'The smoke, the roar and the good-fellowship of relaxed humanity...'

The years he had spent in India had rendered him ill-equipped to withstand the English climate and he could not reconcile himself to the cold winters. 'Once', he wrote, 'I faced the reflection of my own face in the jet black mirror of the window panes for five days'. In 1891 his health broke down, and 'all his Indian microbes joined hands and sang for a month in the darkness of Villiers Street'.

To recuperate, Kipling set off on a tour to Ceylon, Australia, New Zealand and South Africa. For some years he had been friends with an American, Walcott Balestier, to whom he had dedicated *Barrack Room Ballads*. In 1892 Kipling and Balestier's sister, Caroline, were married, and went to live in New England. During the four years they spent there, Kipling wrote *The Jungle Book, Captains Courageous* and *Many Inventions*. They returned to England and lived for three years in a house at Rottingdean, Sussex, until with their daughter Josephine, they returned to America in 1899, where both Kipling and his daughter contracted pneumonia. Both became seriously ill, and within a short time Josephine died. Kipling fortunately recovered and shortly after, he and his wife left America for good. They returned to England and bought 'Batemans' in Burwash, Sussex, which was to remain Kipling's home until his death on January 18th 1936.

 Tube: *Charing Cross.* Circle, District, Northern and Bakerloo Lines.
Bus: Along Strand or through Trafalgar Square. Nos. 6, 9, 11, 13, 15, 77, 176 or 505.

Horatio, Earl Kitchener
2 Carlton Gardens, SW1

Horatio Herbert Kitchener, the great British soldier and statesman, was born in County Kerry on June 24th 1850, the son of a Lieutenant-Colonel. He spent much of his early life in France, where his father was stationed, but returned to England in 1866, staying with George Frost, proprietor of the 'Woolwich Crammer' at Kensington Square, who successfully coached him for the Royal Military Academy at Woolwich, which he entered in 1868.

On gaining his commission as a second lieutenant in 1871, Kitchener spent a short time in France before going on survey expeditions to Palestine and Cyprus between 1874 and 1883. During this time he made regular visits to London, staying at South Kensington.

In 1883 he was promoted to the rank of Captain and attached to the Egyptian army and by 1886 was made Governor-General of Eastern Sudan. Five years later Kitchener became Sirdir of the Egyptian Army and commenced a brilliant military campaign against the Mahdists culminating in their destruction at the Battle of Omdurman in September 1898. Almost overnight Kitchener became a folk hero: he was created Baron Kitchener of Kharthoum and on his return 'every important house in London was tendered as his lodging'. Between the years 1888 and 1914 Kitchener used 17 Belgrave Square as his London address.

After his success in the Middle East, Kitchener, now a Lieutenant-General, was sent to South Africa as Chief of Staff to Field Marshal Roberts in the Boer War. Roberts returned to England in November 1900 and Kitchener succeeded him as Commander-in-Chief. Kitchener brought the war to a relatively successful close in June 1902 and his reputation was further enhanced by the fairness and

moderation of his peace terms.

By now Kitchener had, without question, become the supreme military figure of his time. Returning from South Africa in July, he was made a Viscount and given a grant of £50,000. His stay in England was, once again, short. On October 17th 1902 he left Victoria Station for India as Commander-in-Chief of the East Indies. In 1909, after a somewhat stormy time in India due to friction between Kitchener and the Viceroy to India, Lord Curzon, he was promoted to Field-Marshal and made Commander-in-Chief and High Commissioner in the Mediterranean.

Finally, in 1910, after a period of almost twenty-seven years of constant work, Kitchener had a brief respite and spent the summer and early autumn in country retreats both in England and Ireland.

The following year Kitchener was summoned to London to oversee the military ceremonial for the Coronation of King George V on June 22nd. 'Within an hour of the conclusion of the service in the Abbey, Kitchener, his work done, his reports in, was receiving one or two friends in his flat at Whitehall'. In September he returned to Egypt as British Agent and Consul-General.

In June 1914 he came home on leave, staying at his country home, and receiving an Earldom for his services in Egypt.

On August 2nd, Kitchener left 17 Belgrave Square, and the following day he was crossing the Channel to return to Egypt when Germany declared war on France. Kitchener was recalled immediately and returned to Belgrave Square, where on 6th August he was made Secretary for War. Now based in London, he moved into 2 Carlton Gardens, SW1, loaned to him by Lady Wantage. He resided there until March 6th 1915, when he moved into York House.

Kitchener's 'Your Country Needs You!' recruiting drives are now legendary. His death on June 5th 1916, when the cruiser *Hampshire*, on which he was travelling to Russia for a military conference, was sunk, was a national disaster, and was a major setback to the Allied War effort. His popularity can be gauged by the fact that a Kitchener memorial appeal, headed by the Queen Mother, raised over £700,000.

Tube: *Trafalgar Square.* Bakerloo Line. (A pleasant walk down Pall Mall, which takes only a few minutes.)
Bus: Few buses go along Pall Mall regularly except *westward* by the one way system from Piccadilly and Trafalgar Square i.e. Nos. 9, 14, 506 etc.

57

T. E. Lawrence (Lawrence of Arabia)

14 Barton Street, Westminster, SW1

Born at Tremadoc, North Wales, on 15th August 1888, Thomas Edward Lawrence was one of a family of five sons. His parents were comfortably off and Lawrence was educated at Oxford High School and later at Jesus College, Oxford, where in 1910 he took a first in Modern History. He was subsequently awarded a senior scholarship by Magdalen College which enabled him to spend the next four years assisting Sir Leonard Woolley in the excavation of the Hittite city, Carchemish. During this time he learnt Arabic and acquired the habit of wearing Arab clothes and eating Arab food.

In 1914 Lawrence enlisted in the British Army and was attached to Military Intelligence in Egypt when Turkey joined the enemy alliance. Lawrence subsequently organised the Arab Bureau and acted as intelligence officer during the Arab campaigns. Lawrence was strongly in favour of closer cooperation between the British and the Arabs and he was appointed Adviser and Liaison Officer to the Amir Faisal. Having won Faisal's confidence Lawrence organised his armies so well that in a series of daring military manoeuvres he was able to make large territorial gains for the Arabs against the Turks. He then turned to guerilla train-wrecking sorties and was so successful that a large reward was offered by the Turks for the capture of 'El-Orens, destroyer of engines'.

After the war Lawrence was a leading delegate at the Peace Conference. Disenchanted, however, by his failure to forward Arab interests against the French in Syria, he left the conference table and started writing the story of his adventures.

Returning to England, Lawrence was elected a research fellow of All Souls, Oxford, where he continued his writing. In 1921, at the request of Winston Churchill, he advised on the Middle Eastern settlement but later resigned, disgusted at the Allies' failure to fulfil their moral obligations to the Arabs.

From the beginning of 1922, Lawrence lived in the attic of the office of his friend, the architect Sir Herbert Baker, a three-storeyed brick house built in 1722 (No.14 Barton Street). This provided Lawrence with a much-needed refuge from the glare of publicity surrounding him after his desert exploits. Until enlisting in the RAF in August 1922 (under the name J. H. Ross), Lawrence lived a termitic

existence at Barton Street, sleeping by day and working on the manuscript of his *Seven Pillars of Wisdom* at night. According to Sir Herbert Baker most of the *Seven Pillars* was written at Barton Street, although this statement must be treated with some reservation as other sources indicate that only the final parts and revisions were completed there.

After joining the RAF Lawrence continued to use 14 Barton Street as a forwarding address and occasional residence up to 1929.

The last years of Lawrence's life were unhappy ones, a perpetual flight from his undesired fame. Discharged from the RAF after his identity became known, Lawrence sought refuge in the Tank Corps but later rejoined the RAF. In 1927 he changed his name by deed poll to T. E. Shaw. In March 1935 he retired from the RAF and went to live in Clouds Hill, Bovington, Dorset. Two months later he was dead, killed on May 13th 1935 at Moreton when, in swerving to avoid some children, his beloved Brough Superior motor-cycle hurtled off the road.

Tube: *Westminster.* District and Circle Lines. (Walk past the Abbey and the Houses of Parliament, turn right into Great College Street, and Barton Street is on the left.)
Bus: Past the end of Great College Street. Nos. 3, 77, 77A, 77B, 159 or 168.

Wolfgang Amadeus Mozart
180 Ebury Street, SW1

Leopold Mozart was a musician at the court of the Archbishop of Salzburg. In the summer of 1751, he and his wife Anna had a daughter, Anna Maria, and on January 27th 1756 their second child, Wolfgang Amadeus, was born.

Both children were talented and precocious musicians, and at the age of six Wolfgang wrote his first composition, a concerto for the clavier. An ambitious man, Leopold decided to devote himself to ensuring his children's musical fame; thus in 1762 the family left Salzburg for Vienna, where the two children played to the Emperor and Empress of Austria. Later the Mozarts travelled to France where Wolfgang performed at Versailles before Louis XV.

On April 10th 1764, the strange entourage set off for London. They arrived on the 23rd and obtained lodgings at Cecil Court, St. Martins Lane, with John Couzens, a hairdresser. Three days later the children appeared before King George and Queen Caroline at Buckingham House. Once again they captivated their audience and on 9th May, in the *Public Advertiser,* notice appeared of a performance on the harpsichord at Hickford's Room in Brewer Street, to be given by . . .

'Master Mozart who is a real Prodigy of Nature, he is but seven years of age, plays anything at first sight and composes amazingly well.'

Invited to play again before the King and Queen the Mozarts received from them 24 guineas, a welcome addition to their dwindling finances.

Later that month Leopold became ill and so the Mozarts left London for a short stay in Tunbridge Wells. Returning in August they lodged briefly in Thrift (now Frith) Street, over the shop of a Mr. Williamson, where Wolfgang composed his six sonatas for the harpsichord and violin, as well as a four-part motet.

Shortly after, the Mozart family moved to Five Fields Row in Chelsea, where they lodged with a Dr. Randall in what is now 180 Ebury Street. Leopold Mozart was still very ill and musical instruments were forbidden, in case he was disturbed. Forced to find quieter entertainments, Wolfgang, with the assistance of his sister, composed his first symphony, an incredible achievement for a child of eight. That November, Queen Caroline was presented with the works composed by Wolfgang while at Five Fields Row. The Queen was entranced and gave him a present of fifty guineas. He also gave the British Museum copies of his sonatas and a madrigal. Ending their stay in Chelsea at the end of the year, the family left England for Europe, eventually returning to Salzburg in

November 1766.

The greater part of the remainder of his short life Mozart spent travelling through Europe, achieving great musical acclaim but little financial success.

In 1782 Mozart had married eighteen-year-old Constance Weber. They settled in Vienna where Constance gave birth to a son, Karl. Mozart's health, however, was rapidly deteriorating and by November 1791 he was bedridden. He still continued to work on what was, ironically, to be his final composition, the *Requiem*. On December 4th 1791 Wolfgang Mozart died, leaving to posterity no less than 625 works written during his short life.

Tube: *Victoria*. Circle, District and Victoria Lines. (Off Grosvenor Gardens – a short walk from Victoria Station.)
Bus: 39 or 11 (westward). Get off at Ebury Street, off the Pimlico Road.

Horatio, Viscount Nelson

103 Bond Street, W1

Horatio Nelson's father was rector of the parish of Burnham Thorpe in Norfolk, where Nelson was born on September 29th 1758. After a somewhat desultory education, Horatio entered the navy at the age of twelve as a midshipman on the *Raisonable*.

Nelson's progress was extraordinary: he became a captain at the age of twenty. He gained wide experience in all parts of the world, from the East Indies to Nicaragua, where in 1780 he nearly died from fever. The next year he was appointed to the frigate *Albemarle* and voyaged to Canada where, in Quebec, he became involved in the first of the passionate and consistently impractical love affairs that characterised his entire career.

In 1787 whilst overseeing British naval interests in the West Indies he met Frances Nisbet, a doctor's widow with a young son, and married her on the 12th March.

By now Nelson's characteristic independence of thought and action was fully developed, as well as his fierce nationalistic pride. During the period 1788 to 1800 as captain of the *Agamemnon* he saw almost continual active service, first in the Mediterranean, where in Naples he met Lady Emma Hamilton.

In 1794 he lost his right eye at Calvi when it was pierced by gravel thrown up by a cannonball.

Returning to England in 1796, he took up residence at 96 New Bond Street (now 103), but lived in this house for only two months before leaving on the 29th March 1797 to sail to the south-west coast of Portugal where the Battle of Cape St. Vincent took place. Soon after, in an assault upon Santa Cruz, Nelson suffered the loss of his right arm.

After recovering he sailed early in 1798 for the Mediterranean where he won a barony for his brilliant victory over the French fleet on August 1st as it lay at anchor in Aboukir Bay. Nelson's action cut off Napoleon's eastern army from its European sources of supply and doomed its undertaking to failure.

Nelson was again wounded during the battle, after which he sailed for Naples where he was cared for by Lady Emma Hamilton, who became his mistress, beginning one of the most famous and controversial love affairs in history.

Lord Minto remarked of Nelson that he 'swallowed flattery like a child swallows pap'. His combined passions for flattery and Emma Hamilton led him to commit acts of folly which antagonised both Society and the Admiralty, so that on his return to England whilst he was lionised by the mob he was ostracised by Society, who resented his forcing of Lady Hamilton upon them, and resented even more his callous treatment of his wife.

Nelson lived in a number of houses in London over the years, but 103 New Bond Street is the only surviving

building among them. It is a four-storeyed house, and the proportion and disposition of the windows, three to each storey, suggests that the building is of late eighteenth century origin. Although the original structure has been altered by the insertion of a large shop display window on the ground floor, it is otherwise little changed since Nelson's time.

Nelson was created a Viscount after his victory at Copenhagen, and when on the 20th October 1805 the French and Spanish fleets put to sea, he led the British fleet in the flagship *Victory,* which is still preserved at Portsmouth. It was from this ship that he flew his famous signal 'England expects that every man will do his duty', and in which he died from a bullet wound in the hour of his triumph on October 21st 1805 off Cape Trafalgar.

Tube: *Bond Street.* Circle Line. (A short walk down New Bond Street.)
Bus: No.25 down New Bond Street, or Nos. 1, 6, 8, 12, 13, 15, 73, 88, 113, 137, 159, 500, 505, 616 etc. along Oxford Street.

Sir Isaac Newton

87 Jermyn Street, SW1

Isaac Newton, the greatest of English scientists and philosophers, was born on Christmas Day 1642, at Woolsthorpe in the parish of Colsterworth, Lincolnshire. His father, a farmer, died before Isaac was born. Newton first attended two local village schools, and then the Grammar School at Grantham where, after a slow start, he rose to be head boy. He showed an early aptitude for things mechanical, producing water-clocks, miniature windmills, and even a four-wheeled passenger-propelled carriage.

In 1656 Isaac's stepfather, Barnabas Smith, died, and his mother and her three children by her second marriage returned to Woolsthorpe. At this time Newton left school in order to take up his father's profession of farming. It was soon obvious that the land was not his milieu, and so he returned to school at Grantham.

From there, Newton went up to Trinity College, Cambridge, where he was admitted as a subsizar on 5th June, 1661. At Cambridge his interest in geometry, trigonometry and astronomy flourished, and in January 1665 he took his BA, soon after which he was 'forced from Cambridge by the plague'.

On October 1st 1667 he was elected a Fellow of his College, and on 29th October 1669 he was elected Lucasian Professor.

During the next few years he undertook detailed optical research, and many of his findings were published in the *Philosophical Transactions*.

Newton's attentions were first turned to the subject of gravity whilst he was at Woolsthorpe in 1666. The 'apple' story was subsequently put abroad by Voltaire. Isaac Newton's great work on gravity, *Principia*, was first published in 1687 and caused great excitement throughout Europe.

In 1687 James II unconstitutionally attempted to have a Benedictine monk admitted to Cambridge University as a Master of Arts without taking the Oaths of Allegiance and Supremacy, and Newton was among those called upon to defend the university against the royal action. The defence, before Judge Jeffries, was unsuccessful but led to Newton being elected Member of Parliament for the University in 1689 and taking up residence in London 'at Mr. More's house in the Broad Sanctuary at the west end of Westminster Abbey'. His stay in London was terminated the following year by the dissolution of Parliament, and Newton returned to his rooms in Cambridge. At this time London life does not appear to have impressed him favourably, for he complained of '... *confinement to the London air, and to such a way of living as I am not in love with.*'

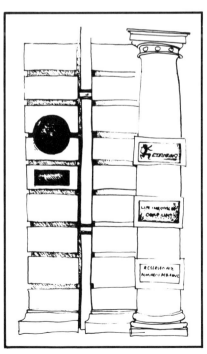

During Newton's first stay in London he formed a close friendship with John Locke, who later tried to obtain for him a post of national importance befitting his stature. In 1694 this was eventually achieved when Charles Montague (later the Earl of Halifax) was appointed Chancellor of the Exchequer. He wrote to Newton:—

'*I am very glad that at last I can give you a good proof of my friendship, and the esteem the King has of your merits. . . .the King has promised me to make Mr. Newton the warden of the Mint. The office is the most proper for you. 'Tis the chief office of the Mint; 'tis worth five or six hundred pounds per annum, and has not too much business to require more attendance than you can spare.*'

Three years later Newton was given the Mastership of the Mint, which carried a salary of £1,500 per annum. He took a house in Jermyn Street, No.87, where he stayed a year before moving to a bigger house next door, No.88, a few steps from his friend Charles Montague.

Jermyn Street was built in about 1667, and was named after Henry Jermyn, the Earl of St. Albans. By 1697 there were 55 houses on the south side, the individual values of each being indicated by their annual sewer rating, which ranged from £10 to £140.

Newton retained his mathematics chair at Cambridge whilst at the Mint until 1701, when he was again elected as a University representative to Parliament until its dissolution the following July. In 1703 he was elected President of the Royal Society, a post he retained until his death, and in 1705 he received a knighthood from Queen Anne.

Newton eventually left Jermyn Street in 1709, but continued his studies into physics, chemistry and theology.

His health remained good until the last few years of his life, when he became incontinent. In 1725 he suffered an attack of gout, and his post at the Mint was taken over by his niece's husband, John Conduitt. He was now living at Kensington, where his health gradually deteriorated, and he died peacefully of 'disease of the stone' on Monday, March 27th 1727, aged 84. 87 Jermyn Street underwent fairly drastic alterations in the 18th and 19th centuries, and was for a time around 1780 used as 'gentlemen's chambers', at which time it is reputed that Lord Nelson occasionally stayed there.

Tube: *Piccadilly Circus.* Bakerloo and Piccadilly Lines. (A very few minutes' walk from the tube station.)
Bus: Along Piccadilly — Nos. 9, 14, 19, 22, 38 or 506 (get off at Piccadilly Circus). Down Regent Street — 3, 6, 12, 13, 15, 39, 53 or 159 (get off at Piccadilly Circus).

Samuel Pepys
12 Buckingham Street, WC2

Samuel Pepys was born on the 22nd February 1633 at Salisbury Court, Fleet Street. His father was a tailor whose ancestors had risen from the position of yeoman farmers to minor gentry.

Pepys was educated at Huntingdon Grammar School and St. Paul's School where, as a fifteen year old, he witnessed the execution of Charles I. From 1650 to 1654 he was an undergraduate at Magdalen College, Cambridge. Soon after leaving, Samuel married fifteen year old Elizabeth St. Michel at St. Margarets, Westminster, and began his career, as a clerk, for his cousin Edward Montagu.

Samuel Pepys is best remembered for his diary which covers the years 1660–1669 and is a frank and fascinating insight into the mind of a restoration sensualist. The diary,

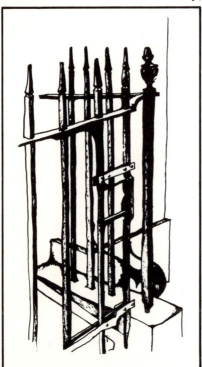

obviously written as a purely personal document, was written in a shorthand code, not deciphered until nearly 120 years after his death.

Until 1660 Pepys lived in a house at Axe Yard, Westminster, whence he moved to an official residence in the Navy Office between Crutched Friars and Seething Lane. In 1673 he was appointed Secretary to the Admiralty and took over part of the Admiralty Office in Canon Row as his home.

Pepys had been a close confidant of the Duke of York (later to become James II) who, in 1672, became a Roman Catholic. This, coupled with the fact that it was thought that Pepys's wife had been converted to Catholicism before her death in 1669, led to his being arrested at the height of the Popish Plot in 1678 on trumped-up charges of betraying naval secrets to the French. Released on bail, Samuel found refuge early in 1679 at 12 Buckingham Street, with his former servant, Will Hewer. Here Pepys *'received from him,* (Hewer) *all the care, kindness and faithfulness of a son'.* Will Hewer had taken possession of the house in 1677 when it was built. In November 1680 the house narrowly escaped being burnt down. Hewer wrote to Pepys who was away, apologising for his delay *'by the disorder that I am put in by an unlucky accident that was (very happily) discovered by our next neighbour . . . of a fire that had been kindling all day under a fire hearth next your Closset and broake out about tenn at night'.* In 1984 the two houses on the other side of Pepys' residence *were* burnt down, and in the confusion Will Hewer had some of his goods stolen.

That same year both Pepys and the Duke of York were restored to royal favour, the king reappointing the latter Lord High Admiral and the former 'Secretary for the Affairs of the

Admiralty of England.'

For the next four years, as well as being the home of Will Hewer and Samuel Pepys, now at the zenith of his career, 12 Buckingham Street became the Admiralty Office. In 1688 Pepys, feeling perhaps that his present home was somewhat lacking in grandeur, moved to No.14, a large river-fronted house on the corner of the street, where he remained until 1701. Hewer retained No.12 for another year, before retiring to Clapham. Pepys too retired to Clapham in 1701 and died there on the 26th May 1703.

14 Buckingham Street has since been rebuilt; No.12, however, remains substantially as it was in Pepys' day, although the front door has been replaced. Inside, the oaken staircase, which Pepys no doubt climbed each night on his way to bed, candle in hand, still remains.

Tube: *Charing Cross.* District, Circle, Bakerloo, and Northern Lines. (A short walk from the station, Buckingham Street runs from the Strand to the River embankment east of the station.)
Bus: Along Strand or through Trafalgar Square. Nos. 6, 9, 11, 13, 15, 77, 176 or 505.

William Pitt (The Younger)
120 Baker Street, W1

William Pitt was born in Hayes, Kent, on May 28th 1759, with a political silver spoon wedged firmly in his mouth. His father, William Pitt (the elder), later to become the Earl of Chatham, was the foremost statesman of his era.

As a child William's mind and body rapidly outstripped his constitution and so, unlike most boys of his age and station, he was not packed off to public school but tutored at home. Many of the eminent people who regularly visited his home were startled by the boy's intellect and at a very early age he acquired a burning fascination for politics. When his father was made Earl of Chatham in 1766, the seven-year-old William commented that he was glad that he was not the eldest son because he wanted to speak in the House of Commons, like his father!

William Pitt entered Pembroke Hall, Cambridge, in 1773, and threw himself into the task of learning with even greater vigour. On leaving University in 1780 Pitt took chambers in Lincoln's Inn and became a barrister. Later that year there was a general election, at which Pitt unsuccessfully stood as candidate for Cambridge University.

The Duke of Rutland, however, through Sir James Lowther ensured Pitt's entry to Parliament by giving him a seat in one of the boroughs under Lowther's control, Appleby in Westmorland. He made his maiden speech on February 26th 1781, and his power of oratory was even then such that Edmund Burke was moved to tears, exclaiming 'It is not a chip off the old block; it is the old block himself'.

Pitt's parliamentary career was, to say

the least, meteoric. He rejected out of hand offers of junior government posts including the Marquess of Rockingham's promise of the Vice-Treasurership of Ireland, until at the age of twenty-three, he accepted the office of Chancellor of the Exchequer, under Shelburne who had succeeded to the premiership on Rockingham's death in 1782. British politics was, at this time, in such a state of flux that a succession of toothless minority governments were formed and fell with monotonous regularity. Pitt, who had supported the unstable and bewildered King George III against the political machinations of Charles James Fox and Lord North, was invited by the King to form a government. Pitt, however, realising that he would not have a Commons majority and that he would lack any effective power, declined, leaving his opponents Fox and North to form a coalition government.

To the King's relief, in November 1783 the new government was defeated over the India Bill and Parliament dissolved. On December 19th Pitt was once again asked to form a new government and so, at the age of twenty-four, William Pitt the younger became Prime Minister of Great Britain. The 'schoolboy prime minister' suffered an immediate Commons defeat but refused to resign, managing to hold the reins of government until a general election gave him a workable majority the following year.

Pitt remained in office continuously from 1783 to 1801 and during that time his London residence was, of course, 10 Downing Street.

Pitt had few close friends, but one of the men closest to him was William Wilberforce (see page 88) the great reformer who, at this time, lived in Wimbledon. This prompted Pitt in August 1784 to lease a small house on the north side of Putney Heath, which enabled him to benefit from the country air without neglecting his state duties.

In 1785 Pitt purchased a country estate, Holwood Hill near Bromley, Kent, 'a most beautiful spot wanting nothing but a house fit to live in'. The purchase of Holwood Hill placed Pitt, by no means a wealthy man, in a precarious financial position from which he never really recovered.

Despite scathing comments from Fox and North about the 'schoolboy prime minister' and Fox's prediction that Pitt's administration would collapse within a fortnight, Pitt remained in office for over sixteen years, until his resignation in February 1801 over the Catholic Emancipation Bill, having weathered the not inconsiderable storms of the American War of Independence and the French Revolution.

In 1798 Pitt, after a heated Commons exchange with George Tierney, was challenged by the latter to a duel. The match took place on May 27th at Putney Heath, near to where the Portsmouth Road joins Kingston Vale. Both men fired twice but neither, mercifully, was hit and honour was satisfied. Contemporary wits remarked that since Tierney was twice the size of Pitt, Pitt's figure should have been chalked on Tierney and no shot made by Pitt outside the chalkmark should count!

On March 14th 1801, Pitt resigned his Premiership over the King's refusal to ratify the Catholic Emancipation Bill. Leaving the Prime Minister's official residence at Downing Street, Pitt took a lease on a small furnished house, No.12 Park Place, which had previously been occupied by one of the Under-Secretaries of State. On June 24th 1802 in a letter to Addington accepting a dinner engagement, Pitt wrote, *'Perhaps if you should have no particular use for your carriage and horses, you would let it be in Park Place a quarter before six to convey me . . .'*

Pitt remained at Park Place until the dissolution of Parliament on the 29th June. The summer and autumn of that year were spent at his residence as

Lord Warden of the Cinque Ports, at Walmer Castle, *'gaining a great deal of health and strength by riding and sailing...'*

Pitt, as indicated by his need to borrow Addington's carriage, was in pretty desperate financial straits, his debts now totalling £45,000. Now he was no longer in power his creditors became increasingly insistent and... *'his houses were in danger of being stripped of their furniture, and his stables of their horses.'*

His lease of the house in Park Place having come to an end, he took another, equally small, in the autumn of 1802 – 14 York Place, Portman Square. On the 18th October 1802 the Duke of Orleans wrote to Pitt that... *'on a false report that you was in town I called this morning at your house in York Place, to request an interview with you.'* In fact despite being in possession of York Place at this time, it seems that he did not make his residence there until January 1803, on his return from a 'cure' at Bath. That year too he alternated between Walmer Castle and York Place, and in deference to his financial plight, Holwood was finally sold. An interesting sidelight on Pitt's finances are the weekly food accounts still existing from his residence at York Place, showing a consumption of nearly half a ton of meat each week! It is possible that, unable to afford a reliable steward to administer his domestic affairs, Pitt was being defrauded by his staff. On May 20th Pitt took his seat for the first time in the new Parliament, shortly afterwards making one of his finest speeches, in support of a war with France. In August Pitt's eccentric niece, Lady Hester Stanhope, came to live at York Place henceforth sitting at 'the head of his table'.

The following year, Addington, who had succeeded Pitt as Premier in 1801, went out of office and on May 7th the Earl of Malmesbury, then Lord Chancellor, called on William Pitt. In his own words, *'... the King was just recovered from mental indisposition. He ordered me to go to Mr. Pitt with his commands for Mr. Pitt to attend him. I went to him to York Place to deliver these commands, I found him at breakfast.'*

Pitt immediately reconstructed the Ministry. Malmesbury's diary notes: *'May 15th 1804. Early with Pitt in York Place.'* The last record of his residence there is a letter to Lord Pelham dated May 19th.

Soon after he again took up residence at Downing Street. Now 45, Pitt, whose constitution had never been strong, was suffering from rapidly deteriorating health, made worse by Parliament's impeachment of Melville against his wishes, and the disastrous defeat of the Allied armies by Napoleon at Austerlitz. Legend has it that the ailing Pitt, convalescing at Shockerwick House, on receiving news of Austerlitz, located the village on a map of Europe and bid his host: *'Roll up that map: It will not be wanted these ten years.'*

On January 6th 1806, Pitt left Bath for London, returning to Bowling Green House, Putney Heath, which he had leased eighteen months earlier. On the 12th he wrote to Marquess Wellesley, *'I am recovering rather slowly from a series of stomach complaints, followed by severe attacks of gout, but believe I am now in the way of real amendment.'* He was, however, mistaken and in the early hours of January 23rd 1806, ironically the twenty-fifth anniversary of his entry into Parliament, William Pitt died. His last words, *'My country! How I leave my country!'*

Tube: *Baker Street.* Circle, Metropolitan and Bakerloo Lines.
Bus: Buses only run from North to South down Baker Street. Nos. 1, 2, 13, 26, 30, 59, 74, 74B, 113, 159.

George Bernard Shaw
29 Fitzroy Square, W1

Shaw was Irish, and he was also a vegetarian, facts which may possibly be of significance to the life of this gifted but undeniably eccentric playwright. He was born in Dublin on July 26th 1856, the son of a family of landed gentry that had seen better days. Not a notable scholar, he nevertheless had a flair for composition and his mother, a good amateur singer, gave him 'voice culture' lessons which were to stand him in good stead in later years.

Shaw's mother, together with his two sisters, Lucinda and Elinor (who died in 1876) moved to London in 1872, and four years later, after he had worked for five years in the office of a Dublin estate agent, Shaw joined them at 13 Victoria Grove (now Netherton Grove) off the Fulham Road, where they lived until early in 1882. During this period, apart from a short spell with the Edison Telephone Company, Shaw remained blissfully unemployed. He wrote a series of novels consistent only in the indifference with which they were greeted by London's publishing houses. Later however they were resurrected and used in the various socialist magazines with which Shaw became involved. In 1882 the Shaw family moved to lodgings at 36 Osnaburgh Street, St. Pancras, where they remained for five years, until they took rooms in the more fashionable West End of London, at No.29 Fitzroy Square.

Shaw had been a member of the Fabian Society (curiously described in the Encyclopaedia Britannica as 'a revolting sect from the Fellowship of the New Life'!) for some years and his prodigious output of novels and plays continued, but it was not until 1895 that he achieved his real breakthrough, strangely enough as dramatic critic of Frank Harris's *Saturday Review*. While at Fitzroy Square, Shaw wrote *The Philanderer, Mrs. Warren's Profession, Arms and the Man, The Man of Destiny* and *Candida*.

In 1897 arch-socialist Shaw had become a member of the St. Pancras Parish Council, serving until late 1903, during which time he was a vociferous and outspoken campaigner for improving the lot of the poorer classes. By the turn of the century Shaw was a major force in the literary world, his reputation ever-increasing, his plays, once banned for their daring content, playing to packed houses and in 1925 he was awarded the Nobel Prize for Literature.

In 1898 he married an Irish heiress, Charlotte Payne-Townshend and left Fitzroy Square for a house in the country. Shaw now lived permanently in the country, although from 1899 he had a London pied-a-terre at 10 Adelphi Terrace. Shaw and his wife had for their country home a beautiful house in Ayot-St.-Lawrence, Herts, where he died at the age of 94, on November 2 1950. The house still stands and is open to the public as a Shaw museum.

Of Shaw's addresses, both 13 Victoria Grove and 36 Osnaburgh Street were subsequently demolished and are, respectively, the sites of a nurses' home and an office block. Fortunately 29 Fitzroy Square, pictured above, still stands, little changed from the time of Shaw's residence in the 1880's.

🚇 Tube: *Warren Street*. Victoria Line. (Walk South along Tottenham Court Road, turn right into Warren Street. Warren Street leads into Fitzroy Square.)
Bus: 176.

Mark Twain
(Samuel Langhorne Clemens)
23 Tedworth Square, Chelsea S.W.3

Florida, Minnesota, was the birthplace of Samuel Langhorne Clemens, better known as 'Mark Twain', America's most famous humorous novelist. He was born on November 30th 1835, the son of 'Judge' Clemens, an easy-going storekeeper-cum-lawyer.

When Samuel was four, the family moved to Hannibal on the Mississippi River where, despite little formal education, he eventually became assistant to his brother on the *Hannibal Journal*. He subsequently left to become a journeyman printer, travelling widely across the U.S.A.

Returning to the Mississippi at the age of nineteen, Clemens set about realising his childhood ambition to become a river pilot.

The Civil War brought his days as a river pilot to a premature end, so he and his brother went gold-mining in Carson City, their experiences providing much humour but little money. Ex-gold-miner Clemens then returned to journalism, writing under the sobriquet 'Mark Twain' in the Virginia City *Enterprise* before moving to San Francisco. Here he published his first novel *The Celebrated Jumping Frog of Calveras County*, and found himself a celebrity overnight.

Soon after, in 1870, he married Olivia Langdon. He continued his new career as an author with a string of successful books including *Roughing It, Tom Sawyer, A Tramp Abroad, Life on the Mississippi* and *Huckleberry Finn*.

By now rich as well as famous, he invested heavily in the 'Charles L. Webster Company' which was for a time spectacularly profitable, but later failed even more spectacularly, leaving Twain with immense debts.

With the purpose of earning the money to repay his debts, Twain set off on an extended tour of Europe in 1891. He arrived in England in the autumn of 1896 and moved with his family into a Victorian house in Chelsea – No.23 Tedworth Square. This house was to be Twain's refuge from his grief over the death of his daughter Susy. A. B. Paine (Twain's biographer) wrote:—

'They did not wish to be visited: they did not wish their whereabouts to be known, except to a few of their closest friends; they wanted to be alone with their sorrow...'

Twain's reticence led to a report being circulated that his family had deserted him and that, alone and ill and in poverty, he was labouring to repay his debts. This, like the Associated Press report of his death, proved to be 'an exaggeration'. A nephew, visiting him at Tedworth Square, found him in good spirits, in comfortable surroundings, and in the bosom of his family.

After a short stay in a rented flat at 30 Wellington Court, Albert Gate, Regents Park, Twain and his family returned home to America, his debts paid.

Now a world celebrity and a national institution, Mark Twain returned briefly to England in 1907, where he was made an Honorary Doctor of Literature at Oxford University.

His final home was 'Stormfield', a picturesque country house built for him at Redding, Connecticut, where he died in 1910. Mark Twain's New York home was recently demolished: fortunately 23 Tedworth Square is still standing, unaltered from the time of his residence there.

⬤ **Tube:** *Sloane Square*. District and Circle Lines.
Bus: Best by bus from Victoria (No.39) – get off at Smith Street.

H.G. Wells
13 Hanover Terrace, Regents Park, NW1

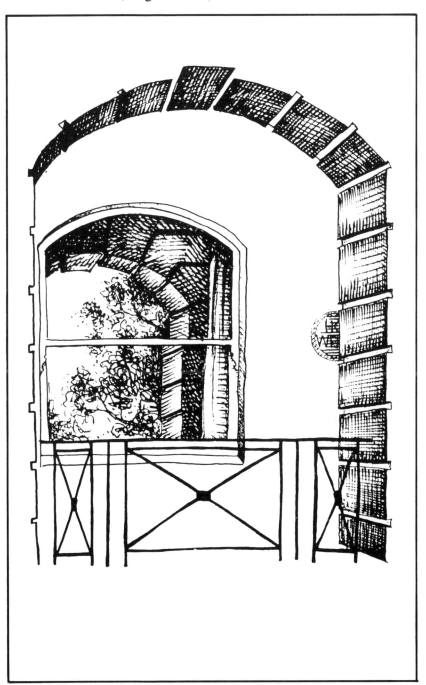

Herbert George Wells, perhaps the most accurately prophetic author of all time, was born unromantically over a china shop in Bromley High Street, on September 21 1866. The child of a broken marriage, 'Bertie' left home at the age of fourteen, taking a rapid succession of jobs before securing a student teachership at a small grammar school. From here he obtained a scholarship to the Normal School (now the Royal College) of Science, where he obtained a first-class honours degree in zoology in 1888.

Wells, a shy, lonely and romantic young man, lodged with his Aunt Mary at 181 Euston Road. Wells, having little contact with women, made his aunt's daughter Isabel the focus of his romantic fantasies. On October 31st 1891 Wells and Isabel were married and moved into 28 Haldon Road, Wandsworth. The marriage was a total disaster and in 1893 Wells left his wife, and went to live with one of his students, Catherine Robbins, at lodgings in 7 Mornington Place, NW1. Isabel eventually divorced Wells and he married Catherine, who subsequently bore him two sons.

By this time he had forsaken academic life for journalism and in 1894 published *The Time Machine*, which was an enormous success. This was followed by a rapid string of novels, including *The Wonderful Visit, The Hand of Dr. Moreau, The Invisible Man* and *War of the Worlds*. Wells soon became a leading member of the literary set of the '90s who found expression in the Fabian Society. His outspoken public and less-than-private life was the cause of much criticism from his contemporaries in the Fabian Society, including Shaw.

From 1909 to 1912 Wells lived with Catherine at 17 Church Row, Hampstead, during which time *The History of Mr. Polly, The New Machiavelli* and *Marriage* were published.

Wells' prodigious and diverse literary output continued: the horrific aerial combats of World War I were prophesied in *War in the Air* published in 1908, the atom bomb in *The World Set Free* published in 1914, and the Second World War in *The Shape of Things to Come* published in 1933.

In 1936 Wells went to live at 13 Hanover Terrace, which he described as 'an old tumble-down house on the border of Regents Park'. It was in fact situated in one of the beautiful terraces on the western side of Regents Park, built in 1822–3 to the designs of John Nash. Wells loved the house: he took a fiendish delight in its number and had a huge figure 13 put up by the door. Wells stayed on in the house right through the war years, refusing to move to the country. Both the house and Wells survived the war, the latter however for little more than a year, dying at Hanover Terrace at the age of 79 on August 13 1946.

Tube: *Regents Park.* Bakerloo Line.
Great Portland Street. Metropolitan and Circle Lines. (A very short walk into and up the east side of the Park.)
Bus: Along Marylebone Road – Nos. 18, 27, 30 or 176, or up Albany Street – Nos. 3 or 53 from Oxford Circus or Regent Street.

13 Hanover Terrace, H. G. Wells' home from 1936 until his death.

James Abbott McNeill Whistler
96 Cheyne Walk, SW3

James Abbott McNeill Whistler was born at Lowell, Massachusetts, on July 10th 1834. His father was a West Point officer turned railway engineer and much of young Jimmy Whistler's childhood was spent in St. Petersburg, his father having been commissioned by the Tsar to build a railway from Moscow to St. Petersburg. Here James learnt to speak French, the language of the Russian aristocracy, and he had his first formal art lessons at the Imperial Academy of Fine Arts.

He visited England briefly in 1846, and the following year he returned for a longer stay, spending nearly a year with his sister and brother-in-law at No. 42 Sloane Street, SW1.

He returned to America with his family in 1849, and after two more years at school entered West Point, though he was eventually expelled for breaches of discipline. He then had a brief spell with a locomotive works in Baltimore before obtaining a post with the U.S. Coast and Geodetic Survey. Here Whistler learned the technique of etching which he was to develop and put to such effect a few years later; it was also here that he realised that any future existence other than as an artist would be unacceptable.

In February 1855 he resigned his U.S. Survey post, and armed with an annual allowance of $350 from his half-brother John, set off to Paris where he spent the next four years studiously avoiding any formal training, learning from his own experience and from his contemporaries including Poynter, Legros, Fantin-Latour and Du Maurier.

In 1859 Whistler tired of Paris and came to London, where he and his brother-in-law Seymour Haden (himself an amateur etcher and artist of considerable talent) went on artistic expeditions together. Whistler also completed the first of his paintings of his sister and niece *At the Piano*. Rejected by the Paris Salon of 1859, the picture was accepted by the Royal Academy in London the following year.

Whistler, excited by the opportunities that seemed open to artists in England, wrote to his friend Fantin-Latour in Paris: *'Come, come, come. Come at once to my house* (i.e. the Haden's house at Sloane Street). *There you will find everything necessary. England, dear friend, greets young artists with open arms.'*

By this time Whistler was becoming increasingly interested in painting as opposed to etching and as the facilities for painting at the Hadens' were limited and his relationship with his brother-in-law was deteriorating, he rented a one-room studio in Newman Street, which became known for *'the noise and the laughter, the lulls for comic anecdotes and the outbursts that followed, the suggestions of capsized furniture and chases round the room.'*

In 1862 Whistler made the acquaintance of D. G. Rossetti, the moving spirit of the Pre-Raphaelite Brotherhood. Rossetti, following in the footsteps of Turner and Carlyle, decided that the rural beauty of Chelsea would be a suitable retreat and took a house there, No. 16 Cheyne Walk. Whistler was most impressed by the house and its location and so took rooms in nearby Queens Road (now Royal Hospital Road). Shortly after he moved to Lindsey House in Lindsey Row (now 101 Cheyne Walk), a mansion originally built by Sir Theodore Mayerne, Court Physician to James I and Charles I. It was subsequently bought by Robert, Earl of Lindsey, and rebuilt by him in 1688. In 1750 a Mansard roof was added and around 1775 the house was subdivided into six separate dwellings and it was into one of these that Whistler moved. In complete contrast to the then current Victorian predeliction for rooms cluttered with furniture, thick carpets and bric-a-brac, Whistler's house had little furniture, matting on the floors, and a small number of paintings and ornaments carefully chosen and subtly placed to complement their surroundings.

It was around this time that Whistler was first attracted by Japanese art, gradually acquiring a superb collection of *objets d'art* including porcelain, fans and woodcuts. The decor of the house became increasingly oriental in style. Whistler's paintings too were noticeably influenced by oriental art, though more in execution than style.

In 1865 Whistler, quite out of the blue, sailed to Valparaiso to offer his services to the Chileans in their fight against the Spanish. It appears he saw little military action during his expedition, but he painted several scenes of Valparaiso's harbour which have since become among the most famous of his works.

After nine months in South America Whistler once again returned to London, leasing another house in Lindsey Row, this time No.2 (now 96 Cheyne Walk), in which he was to live until 1878. The twelve years Whistler lived at No.2 Lindsey Row were possibly his most prolific. The works he produced there included portraits of his mother and Thomas Carlyle, his *Symphony in White No. III*, the series of *Nocturnes,* and several Japanese-inspired canvasses including *Variations in Blue and Green* and *The Balcony*, as well as his *Harmony in Grey and Green,* for which his model, nine-year-old Cecily Alexander, was made to endure over 70 sessions.

No.2 Lindsey Row was the scene of Whistler's famous 'Sunday breakfasts', to which the artist often invited up to twenty people. They were scheduled to start at midday, but Whistler rarely put in an appearance before 2 p.m. However, his conversation, his anecdotes, his histrionic wine-pouring and his buckwheat cakes invariably soothed his impatient guests.

Another oft-repeated incident had Whistler painting in the second-floor studio, one evening, by the light of a candle held by his neighbour, Walter Greaves, when an irate art dealer, to whom Whistler owed money, burst into the room demanding payment.

'Ah, the very man I want' exclaimed Whistler, quite unpeturbed. 'Hold a candle'. Taken aback, the dealer dutifully held a candle until Whistler had finished, whereupon the artist snatched up his canvas and disappeared into the night, leaving the bemused dealer, still unpaid, clutching his candle!

In the mid-1870's Whistler's thoughts turned increasingly to the creation of a 'school' and so he decided to build a fine new house in which his dream

could be realised. He engaged the services of E. W. Godwin, the architect, and a site was found in Tite Street, SW3 (No.48). A three storey house was designed, with a studio comprising the top floor and the 'school' the second. The exterior, which was totally un-Victorian in style, was so simple that the Board of Works insisted upon decorative mouldings being added to keep up the tone of the neighbourhood! It was painted white, roofed with green tiles and was called, predictably, 'The White House'.

The expenses incurred in the building of 'The White House' could not have come at a worse time. In July 1877 John Ruskin, the most influential figure in English art, criticised Whistler's paintings in highly derogatory terms. Whistler was incensed by this unmerited attack and sued the critic for £1,000. When the trial was eventually heard Whistler won his case but was awarded derisory damages and had to pay half the court costs. This was a disastrous blow and on May 8th 1879 he declared himself bankrupt. On September 17th 'The White House' and its contents had to be auctioned (it was, ironically, bought by an art critic) — a sad end to Whistler's grand dream.

At this juncture, the low-point of Whistler's career, he was commissioned by the London Fine Art Society to make a series of twelve etchings of Venice, which together with a set of pastels he produced proved to be an enormous success, earning sufficient to restore the artist to solvency.

Left without a London home and saddened by his mother's death a few months before, in January 1881 Whistler rented No.13 Tite Street, a stone's throw from 'The White House'. In 1886 E. W. Godwin died. Whistler had long been an admirer of Godwin's wife, Beatrix, and in 1888 he disentangled himself from his long-standing mistress Maud Franklin and married Godwin's widow. In 1892 Whistler tired of London and he and his wife went to live in Paris, but after only two years there it was clear that Beatrix's health was failing, and so they returned to England. However, Beatrix's health grew worse and she was moved to a nursing home on Hampstead Heath where she died of cancer on May 10th 1896.

Whistler, in a distraught mood, left England again, but returned when William Heinemann invited him to share his flat in Whitehall Court. Despite Whistler's irascibility, the relationship remained amicable and Whistler stayed at the flat for some while.

In 1902 he returned to Chelsea, his spiritual home, living at No.74 Cheyne Walk where he was looked after by his late wife's sister and her mother. Flashes of the Whistler of old returned when he threatened to sue his next door neighbours, whose house repairs were creating excessive noise. He continued to paint but his strength was ebbing. He died at Cheyne Walk on July 17th 1903 and was buried alongside his wife in Chiswick cemetery.

Tube: *Sloane Square.* District and Circle Lines. Walk along the Kings Road until you come to Beaufort Street on your left. Turn into Beaufort Street and walk along it until you come to Albert Bridge. Cheyne Walk is on the north side of the bridge, on the right.
Bus: Nos. 19, 19A, 39, 39A, 45, 49 or 249 to Battersea Bridge (North Side). Cheyne Walk is to the east of Battersea Bridge, on the Embankment (two minutes' walk).

William Wilberforce
44 Cadogan Place, Chelsea SW1

William Wilberforce's ancestors were landed gentry, who since the reign of Henry II had owned the manor of Wilberfoss in Yorkshire. Wilberforce was born on August 24th 1759 at Hull; when he was nine his father died and he was cared for for the next three years by an uncle at Wimbledon, before returning to Hull. In October 1776 he entered St. John's College, Cambridge, by which time both his uncle and grandfather had died, leaving him heir to a sizeable fortune. In consequence (to his subsequent regret), he did not put in quite the wholehearted academic effort that he might. While at Cambridge he became friendly with William Pitt (see page 73). After leaving University, Wilberforce was elected MP for Hull and soon became a member of the young political 'fast set' in London. However, at the age of twenty-five Wilberforce's life style changed. During a visit to Nice he was converted to evangelicalism by Dr. Isaac Milner, once one of his teachers, and became keenly involved in social reforms. In 1787 he founded the 'Proclamation Society' for the suppression of vice and began his forty-six year battle for the abolition of slavery.

Wilberforce moved into a house in Battersea Rise in 1792, living there until 1797 when he married Barbara Spooner. He and his bride moved to Broomfield, in Clapham, where he became a leading light of the Clapham Sect', a group of Evangelicals living in the area.

His fight against slavery continued. The first great step in Wilberforce's fight against slavery was the Act abolishing the slave trade, which was passed in 1807.

In 1824 he moved to 'The Chestnuts' on Honey Croft Hill, Uxbridge. Retiring from politics the following year, he only remained at 'The Chestnuts' for a short time before retiring to Highwood Hill, near Mill Hill in North London. By 1831 his health was deteriorating and so he moved once again, this time to 9

North Parade, a Regency terrace in Bath. Now seventy-three, Wilberforce was stricken with an attack of influenza and in July 1833 he came up to London to consult his physician.

Mrs. Lucy Smith, his cousin, lent Wilberforce her house, No.44 Cadogan Place, into which he moved on July 9th. Unfortunately, the illness proved too much for him and on July 29th he died. Ironically the culmination of Wilberforce's life work, the Emancipation Act, abolishing slavery in British possessions, was passed in August 1833, a month after his death.

The interior of 44 Cadogan Place is largely unchanged from when William Wilberforce died there. It is a late Georgian house – an extra storey was added in about 1850 and the façade modified by the addition of Italianate stucco ornamentation, then much in vogue.

Tube: *Sloane Square.* Circle and District Lines. (A very short walk from the Tube Station.)
Bus: Nos. 11, 19 or 22 from Knightsbridge, past Sloane Square and into the Kings Road.

Oscar Wilde
34 Tite Street, SW3

Oscar Fingall O'Flahertie Wills Wilde was born in Dublin on October 15 1856. His father, Sir Thomas Wilde, was a surgeon of eminence, and his mother, Jane Francesca Elgee, a writer and poet of some local renown.

Oscar was educated at Portora Royal School at Enniskillen, alongside his elder brother Willie, and he won an Exhibition to Trinity College, Dublin, at the age of seventeen. At Trinity he won the gold medal for Greek, as well as a classical scholarship to Magdalen College. In 1878 Wilde took a first in Moderations and Literae Humaniores, and won the Newdigate prize for his poem *Ravenna*.

It was at Oxford that Wilde first cultivated his pose as an 'aesthete', while his interest in drama as well as his reputation as a conversationalist and wit also flourished amid Arnold's 'dreaming spires'.

On leaving Oxford, Wilde moved to London, taking lodgings at Salisbury Street, near the Strand. He worked as a journalist while preparing a book of poems for publication. Although not an immediate literary success, Wilde was a veritable shooting star in the social firmament, considerably helped by the prominence given to his doings in the society paper *The World*, of which Willie, his brother, was editor. Wilde, the self-styled 'Professor of Aesthetics and Critic of Art' was rapidly becoming a Society cult. *Punch* poured scorn upon what it called 'The Too Utterly Utter' in articles such as the following, published under the title of *A Poet's Day*:

'*Oscar at Breakfast! Oscar at Luncheon!!*

Oscar at Dinner!!! Oscar at Supper!!!!

'*You see I am, after all, mortal' remarked the poet, with an ineffable, affable smile, as he looked up from an elegant but substantial dish of ham and eggs. Passing a long willowy hand through his waving hair, he swept away a stray curl paper, with the nonchalance of a D'Orsay.*

After this effort Mr. Wilde expressed himself as feeling somewhat faint, and with a half-apologetic smile ordered another portion of ham and eggs.'

Money, unfortunately, did not accompany fame, although Wilde's book of poetry appeared in 1881, easing his financial problems. In December he left London for a lecture tour in America, remarking on his arrival, 'I have nothing to declare except my genius'. He returned in April 1883 and the following year married Constance Lloyd. They moved into No.34 Tite Street, a modest house which, however, achieved a certain fame for the eccentricity of the decorations, especially the drawing-room, which incorporated red peacock feathers in the ceiling! The interior was allegedly the work of Whistler, although this is unlikely as he and Wilde had quarrelled the previous year. Frank Harris (not famed for his veracity) assures us that the house was, in fact, decorated by William Godwin.

It was not until 1888 that Wilde's literary career really began to flourish with the publication of *The Happy Prince and Other Tales*. The same year he took on the editorship of the *Lady's World* at a salary of six pounds a week, commuting daily from Tite Street to the editorial offices in Charing Cross. He changed the magazine's name to *Woman's World* and scored an immediate success.

In 1891 Wilde's *Picture of Dorian Gray* was published, followed by a string of successful plays, including *Lady Windermere's Fan* and *A Woman of No Importance*. In 1898 the controversial *Salome* was published, with illustrations by Aubrey Beardsley (see page 9)

In 1894, at the height of his fame, Oscar Wilde fell foul of the Marquis of Queensberry, who resented Wilde's association with his son, Lord Alfred Douglas. Queensberry called on Wilde at Tite Street, and after a blazing row Wilde, pointing at the Marquis, turned to his servant and said 'This is the Marquis of Queensberry, the most infamous brute in London. You are never to allow him to enter my house again'.

After continued goading from Queensberry, Wilde foolishly sued him for criminal libel. The trial took place on April 3rd 1895, and in the face of some highly dubious defence evidence, Wilde lost his case. The 'facts' revealed during the case led to Wilde being tried under the Criminal Law Amendment Act and on May 25th 1895, he was sentenced to two years' hard labour.

Before the trial the contents of Wilde's house in Tite Street were sold to raise money. In the disorder of the auction the house was virtually ransacked and many valuable manuscripts lost or destroyed.

After leaving prison Wilde, a broken man, moved to the Continent, supported by a small income from his wife and a few friends. His last work, *The Ballad of Reading Gaol,* was published in 1898 and he died in Paris from meningitis on November 30, 1900.

His writing remains among the cleverest and wittiest in the English language, and the house in Tite Street, except for the interior decor, is much as it was when Oscar Wilde resided there.

Tube: *Victoria.* Victoria, Circle and District Lines. *Then* take a No.39 bus to just past Chelsea Hospital.

Map reference

Page numbers and map reference

6	**Robert, Lord Baden-Powell of Gilwell** 9 Hyde Park Gate, SW7
9	**Aubrey Beardsley** 114 Cambridge Street, SW1
11	**William Bligh** 100 Lambeth Road, SE1
14	**Sir Winston Churchill** 28 Hyde Park Gate, SW7
17	**Robert, Lord Clive of India** 45 Berkeley Square, W1
21	**Charles Dickens** 48 Doughty Street, St. Pancras
24	**Benjamin Disraeli, Earl of Beaconsfield** 22 Theobalds Road, Holborn, and 19 Curzon Street.
28	**George Eliot (Mary Ann Evans)** 4 Cheyne Walk, SW3
31	**Benjamin Franklin** 36 Craven Street, Westminster
34	**Sigmund Freud** 20 Maresfield Gardens, NW3
36	**Mohandas Karamchand Gandhi (Mahatma)** Kingsley Hall, Powis Road, Poplar
39	**David Garrick** 27 Southampton Street, WC2
41	**Sir William Schwenk Gilbert** 39 Harrington Gardens, SW7
43	**William Ewart Gladstone** 11 Carlton House Terrace, SW1
46	**Georg Friedrich Handel** 25 Brook Street, W1
49	**John Fitzgerald Kennedy** 14 Princes Gate, South Kensington, SW7
52	**Rudyard Kipling** 43 Villiers Street, WC2
55	**Horatio, Earl Kitchener** 2 Carlton Gardens, SW1
58	**T. E. Lawrence (Lawrence of Arabia)** 14 Barton Street, Westminster, SW1
61	**Wolfgang Amadeus Mozart** 180 Ebury Street, SW1
64	**Horatio, Viscount Nelson** 103 Bond Street, W1
67	**Sir Isaac Newton** 87 Jermyn Street, SW1
70	**Samuel Pepys** 12 Buckingham Street, WC2
73	**William Pitt (The Younger)** 120 Baker Street, W1
77	**George Bernard Shaw** 29 Fitzroy Square, W1
79	**Mark Twain (Samuel Langhorne Clemens)** 23 Tedworth Square, Chelsea
81	**H. G. Wells** 13 Hanover Terrace, Regents Park, NW1
84	**James Abbott McNeill Whistler** 96 Cheyne Walk, SW3
88	**William Wilberforce** 44 Cadogan Place, Chelsea
90	**Oscar Wilde** 34 Tite Street, SW3

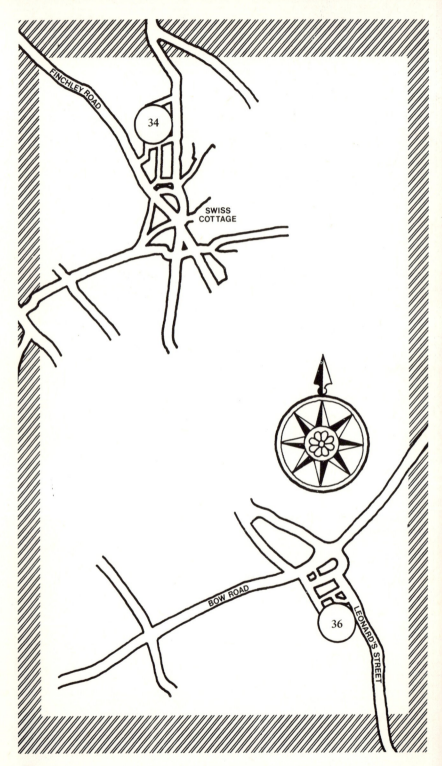